# The Nanotech Revolution Transforming the Future

John Richardson

# Copyright © [2023]

**Author:** John A. Richardson

**Title:** The Nanotech Revolution Transforming the Future

All rights reserved. No part of this publication may be reproduced or transmitted in any form or by any means, electronic or mechanical, including photocopying, recording, or any information storage and retrieval system, without prior written permission from the author.

This book is a self-published work by the author

**ISBN:**

# Table of content

| Chapter name | Page No |
|---|---|
| 1. Nanotechnology: A Brief Overview | 1 |
| 2. Properties of Nanomaterials | 12 |
| 3. Use of Nanotechnology in Healthcare | 22 |
| 4. Electronics and Nanotechnology | 32 |
| 5. Energy and Nanotechnology | 42 |
| 6. The Role of Nanotechnology in Ecological Repairs | 53 |
| 7. The Role of Nanotechnology in Production | 63 |
| 8. Concerns Over the Use of Nanotechnology | 73 |
| 9. Nanotechnology Developments and Prospects | 86 |
| 10. Nanotechnology's Repercussions on Society | 98 |

# Chapter 1.
# Nanotechnology: A Brief Overview

## 1.1- Definition and history of nanotechnology

The Incredible World of Nanotechnology and Its Tiny Wonders

Nanotechnology is an intriguing area of study in science and engineering because it combines elements of science fiction and reality. One billionth of a metre (or nano) is the scale at which nanotechnology operates, which entails the manipulation of matter. Simply said, it's the study and practise of manipulating matter at the atomic and molecular levels to create useful objects. Due to the very small size, hitherto unimaginable qualities and applications are now within reach.

Unlike some other scientific disciplines, nanotechnology didn't spring up out of the ground, but its evolution has been an incredible trip into the ever-shrinking world of the very small. We won't go into the origins of the term nanotechnology, but it's important to recognise how far the field has come in the years since it was coined. However, a firm grasp of what nanotechnology includes is essential before venturing into the technological marvels of today and tomorrow.

What You Need to Know About Nanotechnology's Core Concepts

The ability to control matter at the atomic level is fundamental to nanotechnology. Both top-down and bottom-up approaches can be used for this modification.

Larger constructions or materials can be reduced in size to the nanoscale using top-down nanotechnology. This method is like to chipping away at a block of stone to reveal an intricate sculpture. Lithography and electron-beam machining are two examples of fabrication methods utilised extensively in the semiconductor industry.

Bottom-up nanotechnology, on the other hand, involves constructing something one atom or molecule at a time. Taking this approach is like erecting a structure from the ground up, brick by brick. This strategy relies heavily on chemical synthesis and self-assembly processes. In self-assembly, molecules use their own properties to arrange themselves into predetermined patterns, providing a powerful tool for nanoscale building.

The ability of nanotechnology to take use of quantum effects, the ways in which matter behaves at the atomic and molecular levels, is what sets it apart. Classical physics breaks down in the face of the bizarre and counterintuitive world of quantum mechanics when dealing with such tiny creatures. In the case of electrons, for example, it is possible for them to simultaneously exist in different locations (superposition) and to display correlated behaviour despite their great physical separation (entanglement). To use these events to make new materials and gadgets with remarkable properties is the goal of nanotechnology.

Applications in a Wide Range of Fields

Nanotechnology's wide range of potential uses is one of its most intriguing features. Nanotechnology is a versatile instrument that has the potential to revolutionise many different industries, from health and electronics to energy and environmental cleanup.

Nanotechnology has opened the door to the possibility of precision medicine and the delivery of drugs to specific areas of the body. Drugs can be delivered to the location of disease with minimal adverse effects and maximum therapeutic efficacy by using nano-sized drug carriers. The precision of medical diagnoses has also been improved by nanoscale imaging technologies like quantum dots and magnetic nanoparticles.

Nanotechnology has been the driving force behind the relentless miniaturisation of transistors and circuits in the electronics industry. Nanoscale engineering is responsible for the continued validity of Moore's Law, which asserts that the number of transistors on a microchip will double approximately every two years. New materials and novel ideas, such as quantum computing, promise to revolutionise the electronics industry, however, as we approach the physical limits of silicon-based technology.

Energy is another area where nanotechnology has made an impact. Nanoscale materials and architectures enable highly efficient solar cells, which convert sunlight into power. Nanoparticles are materials that can absorb and convert sunlight with remarkable efficiency, making solar power a more practical and long-term option.

Nanotechnology also has significant applications in environmental cleanup. Pollutants in the air and water can be successfully removed using nanomaterials such synthetic nanoparticles and nanocomposites. They can also be utilised to make manufacturing processes more energy efficient, which in turn reduces the negative effects of manufacturing on the environment.

Quantum Dots and Nanoelectronics: The Quantum Leap

When it comes to nanotechnology, quantum dots are one of the most intriguing breakthroughs. These are nanoscale semiconductor particles with quantum characteristics. Due to a phenomenon called quantum confinement, the size of a quantum dot determines the colour of light it emits. This quality makes them extremely useful in electronic display, lighting, and imaging systems. Quantum dots have been used in state-of-the-art television sets to boost colour saturation and reduce power consumption.

Another major way in which nanotechnology is influencing the electronics sector is through nanoelectronics. Researchers are looking at other materials and methods to continue the miniaturisation trend as traditional silicon-based transistors reach their size limits. Some promising candidates for use in the construction of future electronic devices include carbon nanotubes and graphene, both of which boast outstanding electrical characteristics. Quantum computers, which use quantum bits or qubits, also represent a paradigm shift in computing because they may one day be able to solve problems that are too difficult for classical computers to handle.

Nanomedicine: Internal Health Restoration
Nanotechnology has had a profound impact on medicine, with potential uses in everything from diagnosis to therapy. Nanomedicine, in which nanoparticles are created to interact with the human body at the molecular level, is one of the most promising fields.

Nanoparticles offer unrivalled accuracy in the delivery of drugs. This method of administering medication improves therapeutic efficacy while decreasing unwanted side effects. Cancer treatments, for instance, can be administered specifically to tumours while avoiding surrounding healthy tissue.

The use of nanoparticles has also facilitated the development of cutting-edge imaging methods. High-resolution imaging, early illness detection, and drug distribution tracking are just a few of the applications of nanotechnology like quantum dots and superparamagnetic nanoparticles. In essence, thanks to advancements in nanotechnology, doctors now have access to diagnostic technologies that allow them to see within the human body in ways never before possible.

Even regenerative medicine has felt the impact of nanotechnology. Nanoscale materials can be used to create scaffolds that aid in tissue regeneration and engineering. These components function similarly to the extracellular matrix in the body, guiding the formation of new tissues and organs. This method shows great promise for healing injuries and disorders for which no treatment existed before.

The Future of Nanotechnology and Environmental Sustainability. There has been increasing concern in recent decades about the negative effects of numerous sectors on the environment. Nanotechnology provides novel approaches to addressing these issues, helping to make industries greener and more sustainable.

One such example is the purification of water. Titanium dioxide and silver nanoparticles are only two examples of the nanomaterials used to purify water. Sustainable access to clean drinking water can be ensured by using these materials to degrade organic pollutants and disinfect water.

Nanotechnology has helped enhance renewable energy sources, which is important in the energy business. Nanomaterials like perovskite solar cells enable highly efficient solar cells to absorb light across the electromagnetic spectrum and convert it into electricity at a rate never before achieved. These advancements are lowering the cost and increasing the availability of solar energy.

Nanotechnology has several applications, including in the automotive sector. By using lightweight, high-strength nanomaterials, vehicle fuel consumption and pollutants can be decreased. Additionally, nanotechnology is helping create batteries that are both ecologically benign and efficient for use in electric vehicles.

Issues and Worries

Nanotechnology has enormous potential, but it also comes with a number of risks and worries. Ethical, safety, and regulatory issues are inevitable in any developing field.

## 1.2- Importance of nanotechnology in various industries

The Role of Nanotechnology in Many Fields

Numerous sectors have been radically altered by nanotechnology, the manipulation of matter at the nanoscale, over the past few decades. The fields of medicine, energy, electronics, and materials research can all benefit from it. Nanotechnology has had such a profound effect on various fields that it is now a primary motivator of technological progress. The impact of nanotechnology across industries, and how it will shape the future, are discussed in this article.

Health care (1)

Nanotechnology has had a particularly large impact in the field of medicine. Innovative medical therapies and diagnostic instruments are the primary research interests of nanomedicine, a branch of nanotechnology. Targeted drug administration to specific cells or tissues using nanoscale drug delivery devices, for instance, can lessen adverse effects and increase therapeutic success. These nanocarriers can be customised for sustained medication release, providing continuous treatment.

Nanoparticles are also utilised to improve the contrast and accuracy of medical imaging procedures like MRI and CT scans. Cancer survival rates can be increased if the disease is detected at its earliest, most treatable stage, and this is exactly what researchers have set out to do by developing nanoparticles for early cancer detection. Personalised medicine, in which a patient's treatment is based on their unique genetic makeup, is rapidly progressing because to advances in nanotechnology.

2. electronic gadgets

As a result of advancements in nanotechnology, electronic components may now be made much smaller. As transistors and circuits have shrunk in size, more powerful and efficient electronics have emerged. Microprocessors that have shrunk in size while increasing in speed and efficiency have become indispensable to modern computing and have found use in fields as diverse as aerospace and automotive engineering.

In addition, nanotechnology has allowed for the creation of bendable and wearable electrical devices. Graphene and carbon nanotubes, two types of nanomaterials with exceptional conductivity and mechanical flexibility, play crucial roles in these technologies. This has inspired the development of items like bendable screens, intelligent garments, and portable health trackers.

Third, power.

Nanotechnology is causing a revolution in the energy industry. Nanomaterials, for example, can increase the efficiency of energy conversion in solar cells by enhancing light absorption and electron transport. High-capacity lithium-ion batteries and supercapacitors are only two examples of the energy storage systems that incorporate nanotechnology. These innovations may help us use fewer fossil fuels and mitigate climate change.

Furthermore, nanotechnology is crucial in improving the effectiveness of energy generation and storage infrastructure. It paves the way for the creation of materials that are robust enough to be used in nuclear reactors, wind turbines, and geothermal energy systems, among other places. Improvements in nanotechnology are crucial to the search for greener, more long-term energy sources.

Science of Materials, Number Four
The ability to design and manipulate materials at the nanoscale is what nanotechnology has brought to materials science, and it has

changed the field forever. This has resulted in the development of novel materials with unprecedented characteristics. Nanocomposites, for example, can be designed to have specific properties such as enhanced strength, electrical conductivity, and heat resistance by adjusting the ratio of nanoparticles to matrix.

Coatings and films have also benefited from the advancements made possible by nanotechnology. Surfaces coated with nanoparticles have enhanced scratch resistance, can clean themselves, and are superhydrophobic. These coatings are used in the automotive and aerospace sectors to increase the longevity and efficiency of materials.

Five. Cleaning Up the Environment

The use of nanotechnology is crucial in solving environmental problems. It has been used in the creation of nanomaterials with the ability to purify water and air. To degrade potentially dangerous organic molecules, nanoscale catalysts are utilised in wastewater treatment operations, for instance.

Heavy metals and other poisons can be extracted from polluted areas using nanoparticles. Positive implications for managing pollution at hazardous waste sites and cleaning up industrial and mining areas have been found. Sustainable environmental restoration and lessening the impact of human activity on the world are both goals that can be advanced with the help of nanotechnology.

Aviation and Military Defence Sixth

Nanotechnology has been a game-changer for the aerospace and defence industries by allowing for the creation of superior materials and lightweight, high-performance components. Aircraft and spacecraft made with nanocomposites and nanomaterials are not only more durable but also lighter, which improves their fuel efficiency and decreases their environmental impact.

Sensor, surveillance, and communication system advancements have also resulted from nanotechnology. Nanoscale sensors have the potential to increase the accuracy of a wide range of industries and fields, including the military and the defence sector. Stealth materials and coatings, which make military equipment less visible to radar and other monitoring systems, rely heavily on nanotechnology.

Agriculture, number seven

Nanotechnology's use in farming could help feed a burgeoning world population while reducing agriculture's negative effects on the environment. The use of nanoparticles has the potential to increase crop yields by decreasing fertiliser and pesticide waste.

In addition, nanoscale sensors can track soil moisture and plant vitality in real time, leading to better resource allocation. The use of nanotechnology in precision agriculture has the potential to completely revamp crop production and management, leading to a more environmentally friendly and resilient food system.

Textiles and clothing (No. 8)

Thanks to nanotechnology, the textile and apparel sector is witnessing a period of unprecedented creativity and growth. Fabrics can gain a wide variety of useful characteristics when nanomaterials are woven into them. Nanocoatings, for instance, can be used to impart water and stain resistance to textiles while yet allowing them to breathe. Besides blocking the sun's rays, these materials have other uses, such as fighting bacteria and germs and cleaning themselves.
Smart textiles, which can track physiological data, alter their colour or look, and control temperature, are also being developed with the

help of nanotechnology. These developments not only make clothing more efficient and useful, but they also pave the way for sustainable, environmentally friendly clothing options.

The Food Market

Nanotechnology has had an impact across several industries, including the food production sector. Improved flavour, texture, and visual appeal are just some of the benefits of adding nanoparticles and emulsions to processed foods. Nanoemulsions, for instance, can increase the bioavailability of fat-soluble vitamins in many foods and boost the stability of salad dressings.

The packaging and storage of food also benefit greatly from nanotechnology. Antimicrobial and oxygen-barrier coatings made from nanoscale materials keep food fresher for longer and help keep edibles out of landfills. To further guarantee the quality and safety of the food we consume, nanosensors can identify potential pollutants and diseases.

Tenthly, the Building and Infrastructure Industries

Advances in nanotechnology are being made in the building and infrastructure industries. The use of nanoparticles in self-healing concrete has the potential to greatly increase the durability of structures like bridges and buildings. The development of ultra-resilient, high-performance materials is another area where nanotechnology has made a significant impact.

Nanocoatings are also utilised to prevent surface deterioration due to environmental factors including corrosion and weathering. This can be used to improve the upkeep of bridges and other essential infrastructure like pipelines and historic buildings.

11.1: Space Travel

Nanotechnology has been incredibly helpful for space travel. Spacecraft have utilised miniature instruments and nanosensors to collect data and conduct experiments in space. With the help of these innovations, space exploration missions have become more effective and affordable.

The incorporation of nanotechnology into the design of spacesuits and other hardware has greatly contributed to the improvement of these systems.

# Chapter 2.
# Properties of Nanomaterials

## 2.1- Explanation of different nanomaterials

Nanomaterials with Varying Purposes

Thanks to their nanoscale dimensions, nanomaterials are an intriguing class of materials with novel features and useful uses. Materials of the nanoscale scale have unique physical, chemical, and mechanical properties compared to their bulk counterparts. Scientists and engineers have been able to create and manage a vast range of nanomaterials, each with its own unique features and possible uses, thanks to the development of nanotechnology. The features of nanoparticles and the many areas they have an effect on are discussed in this article.

Nanotubes of carbon

One of the most recognisable nanomaterials is the carbon nanotube (CNT), a cylinder of carbon atoms. Their qualities vary depending on whether they are single-walled (SWCNTs) or multi-walled (MWCNTs). CNTs have extraordinary thermal characteristics, mechanical strength, and electrical conductivity. Because of their unique qualities, they can be used for things like energy storage, building materials, and electronics.

CNTs have been employed as the foundation for flexible, high-performance electronics and as components in transistors and interconnects. As a result of their mechanical strength, they have also been used to reinforce materials for use in things like sports gear, aerospace components, and more. In addition, CNTs have potential use in energy storage technologies including high-capacity batteries and supercapacitors.

Number Two: Graphene

Graphene is yet another nanomaterial based on carbon, but its structure differs from other carbon-based nanomaterials in that it consists of a single layer of carbon atoms. Because of its unique characteristics, it has become one of the most studied and lauded nanomaterials. Graphene is a superb thermal and electrical conductor and has the added benefit of being extremely lightweight.

Graphene could be used in a wide variety of contexts. Because of its higher electrical conductivity and greater mechanical flexibility, it has the potential to displace silicon in many electronic applications. For touchscreens and bendable displays, it is also employed in the creation of transparent conductive films. Composites based on graphene have the potential to improve the strength and thermal qualities of materials used in aerospace, automobile, and building applications.

(3) Quantum Dots

Quantum dots are nanocrystals of semiconductors that exhibit unusual optical characteristics. In applications such as displays, photography, and lighting, their size and composition may be tuned to emit certain wavelengths of light, making them extremely valuable. Colour and efficiency in electronic displays can be improved with the help of quantum dots.

They provide imaging agents in medical imaging with great diagnostic accuracy and monitoring sensitivity. The efficiency of solar panels is being improved by studying the use of quantum dots in photovoltaic cells. The field of optoelectronics stands to benefit greatly from their tunability.

Nanoparticles, number four

Nanoparticles, as a class of nanomaterials, are extremely diverse and can comprise anything from pure metal to metal oxide. They have a wide variety of uses and typically measure less than 100 nm in size. Nanoparticles of some metals, such gold and silver, have interesting optical and catalytic capabilities.

Because of their ability to be tagged with biomolecules for selective delivery to cells and tissues, gold nanoparticles are used in diagnostics and medical imaging. They are also utilised in the treatment of cancer, as they can be used to deliver medications to cancer cells specifically. Silver nanoparticles are widely employed in consumer goods due to their antibacterial qualities; examples include wound treatments, clothing, and cosmetics.

Titanium dioxide and zinc oxide, two common types of metal oxide nanoparticles, are used as UV filters in sunscreens and cosmetics. They're also put to use in high-performance materials research, environmental cleanup, and catalysis.

Nanowires, number five

Nanowires are nanometer-thick, elongated structures. Different materials, including as semiconductors, metals, and even organic substances, can be used to construct them. Because their length is so much greater than their breadth, nanowires have a characteristically high aspect ratio.

Nanoscale transistors, sensors, and integrated circuits are all made possible by the employment of semiconductor nanowires in the realm of electronics. Miniaturised electronic components are made possible by their compact size. In addition, nanowires can be used as components in sensors that detect a wide range of environmental conditions, such as chemicals, temperatures, and pressures.

Nanoporous Materials, Number Six

Nanoporous materials are constructed with pores or spaces at the nanoscale. Molecular or gaseous substances can be absorbed or trapped by the huge surface area of these materials. Activated carbon is a popular nanoporous material used for gas adsorption and purification.

Catalysis and ion exchange are just two of the many uses for zeolites, a type of nanoporous material. They find widespread application in the environmental and petrochemical sectors. More recently, a category of nanoporous materials known as metal-organic frameworks (MOFs) has been discovered. For the purposes of gas storage, separation, and medicine delivery, they are the subject of research.Seventhly, nanocomposites.Nanocomposites are composites made up of a matrix and reinforcing components that are nanoscale in size. These composites feature a matrix material with enhanced properties thanks to the use of nanoscale reinforcements. Polymers, ceramics, and metals can all benefit from having carbon nanotubes or graphene inserted into them to improve their mechanical, electrical, and thermal properties.

Nanocomposites are used to lighten aerospace and automotive components without compromising strength. They're also used to create lightweight, high-strength materials for use in construction and athletic gear.Nanofilms and coatings, number eight

Surfaces can be modified by nanofilms and coatings, which are very thin layers of nanomaterials. Surfaces treated with a superhydrophobic coating, for instance, are highly resistant to water and liquids and may clean themselves. Fabrics, electronics, and building supplies can all benefit from these coatings. Nanoparticles with antimicrobial capabilities are used to cover antibacterial nanocoatings, which can then be used to medical devices, fabrics, and food packaging. Furthermore, solar cells can benefit from the increased light absorption and energy conversion made possible by nanoscale coatings.

Number Nine: Nanoceramics

Ceramics containing nanometer-scale characteristics, such as grain boundaries and pores, are known as nanoceramics. When compared to standard ceramics, these materials are superior in terms of mechanical strength, hardness, and wear resistance. They find use in anything from surgical instruments to tooth implants.

The subject of biomaterials is another area where nanoceramics have found use. They are biocompatible and can merge with the human body, making them useful for bone implants and prosthetics. These materials facilitate efficient integration and regeneration due to their nanoscale structure that mimics that of genuine bone.

Nanofibers, number ten

Nanofibers are extremely thin fibres, typically measuring in the nanometer range. Polymers, carbon, and ceramics are just some of the materials that can be used to create them. Nanofibers are lauded for their superior mechanical qualities and large surface area. Filtration, tissue engineering, and composites are only some of the many uses to which they are put.

Nanofibers can be used to filter out impurities and tiny particles. As a result of their excellent filtration effectiveness and low airflow resistance, they are used in a variety of water and air filtration systems. Nanofibers are utilised as scaffolds in tissue engineering, allowing for cell proliferation and tissue regeneration. Nanoscale dimensions are similar to that of the body's own extracellular matrix, which encourages

## 2.2- Unique properties of nanomaterials and their applications

Nanomaterials' One-of-a-Kind Characteristics and Potential Uses

The extraordinarily tiny size and one-of-a-kind features of nanomaterials have radically altered the fields of science and technology. Materials in the nanoscale have unique physical, chemical, and mechanical properties from those at the bulk scale. These remarkable characteristics have unleashed a flood of new ideas and avenues for exploration in many different sectors. This article delves into the special characteristics of nanomaterials and their many possible uses.

1. Properties That Vary With Size

Nanomaterials are distinguished by size-dependent properties, one of their defining characteristics. New properties of materials at the nanoscale can be used in useful ways. The higher surface area-to-volume ratio is responsible for these size-dependent qualities, since it improves reactivity and other aspects.

Nanoparticles, for instance, are very effective catalysts because their surface area to volume ratio is quite high. The manufacture of chemicals, the refining of petroleum, and the cleanup of polluted environments all rely heavily on the use of catalysts. By offering a bigger and more reactive surface for chemical reactions to occur, nanocatalysts like platinum nanoparticles can greatly improve the efficiency of these processes.

(2) Extraordinary Stability and Resilience

Many nanoparticles also have remarkable durability and strength. Examples of materials with exceptional mechanical qualities include carbon nanotubes (CNTs). Despite their diminutive size, their tensile strengths surpass those of steel. Because of their unique characteristics, CNTs have great potential as composite reinforcements.

CNTs are utilised to make lightweight, high-strength materials that are employed in the aerospace and automobile industries to increase fuel efficiency and decrease pollution. Nanotubes are also used to create lighter and more efficient sporting equipment like tennis rackets and bicycle frames.

Third, improved conductivity (both electrical and thermal)

Enhanced electrical and thermal conductivity are common properties of nanomaterials. Graphene, which consists of a single sheet of carbon atoms organised in a hexagonal lattice, is a good illustration. It conducts heat and electricity exceptionally well. Graphene's exceptional electrical characteristics may cause a seismic shift in the electronics sector.

Graphene's higher electrical conductivity and mechanical flexibility make it a viable alternative to silicon in electronics. Touchscreens and flexible displays that use transparent conductive films are another application. Graphene's usefulness as a thermal interface material and in thermal management for electronic devices is due in no small part to its exceptional heat-conducting properties.

4. Optical Properties That Can Be Adjusted

Nanomaterials' adaptable optical properties make it possible to fine-tune their light-gathering and -emitting capabilities. It is commonly known that quantum dots, nanometer-sized semiconductor nanocrystals, emit light at very particular wavelengths. This quality makes them extremely useful in a wide variety of applications, especially in display, imaging, and lighting.
Displays, such as LCD and QLED televisions, use quantum dots to improve colour and efficiency. In medical imaging, their adaptable

optical properties are used to create diagnostic and monitoring tools with superior resolution and sensitivity. Furthermore, quantum dots' employment in photovoltaic cells shows promise for enhancing solar panels' performance.

5. Improved Magnetism

The improved magnetic properties of certain nanoparticles have potential uses in domains such as data storage and biomedicine. Engineered to have certain magnetic properties, magnetic nanoparticles find use in many fields.

High-density magnetic storage medium, including hard drives and magnetic cassettes, rely on magnetic nanoparticles to store digital information. They are able to store massive amounts of data in small packages because of their small size and magnetic characteristics. Medical applications for functionalized magnetic nanoparticles include targeted medication administration and MRI contrast agents. They improve the quality of MRI scans and allow for targeted drug delivery to specific tissues or cells.

6. Self-Cleaning and Superhydrophobic Characteristics

The superhydrophobicity of surfaces can be engineered into nanomaterials through a variety of methods. Nanostructured coatings or surface textures are used to provide this property by trapping air and preventing water from adhering to the surface. Amazing uses for superhydrophobic coatings can be found in construction, transportation, and consumer goods.

Using superhydrophobic coatings, architects can make surfaces that don't show dirt and water as easily. Car manufacturers use these coatings on windows and bodywork to increase visibility and prevent dirt buildup. Superhydrophobic coatings are also applied to consumer goods like garments to make them waterproof and resistant to stains.

## Method 7: Selective Adsorption/Filtration

The selective adsorption and filtration capabilities of nanoporous materials are unparalleled. In order to adsorb desired molecules or trap desired particle sizes, these materials are designed with tunable pore diameters and surface chemistry.

Activated carbon is a popular nanoporous material for purifying and adsorbing gases. It is commonly used in systems that disinfect air and water by filtering out harmful gases, odours, and other impurities. Another type of nanoporous material with applications in the petrochemical and environmental sectors is zeolites, which are valued for their ion exchange and catalytic qualities. One relatively new type of nanoporous material being investigated for use in gas storage, separation, and medication delivery is metal-organic frameworks (MOFs).

Biodegradability and Specific Drug Delivery is Topic No. 8.

The biocompatibility of several nanomaterials makes them ideal for usage in healthcare settings. In order to deliver drugs specifically to cells or tissues, biocompatible nanomaterials can be functionalized with these molecules.

For instance, gold nanoparticles find extensive use in the medical field. They can be modified with biomolecules to specifically target cancer cells, transport medications, and boost therapeutic efficacy with minimal side effects to healthy tissue. The potential benefits of this targeted medication delivery method for cancer treatment and the mitigation of chemotherapy's side effects are enormous.

## 9. Environmental Cleanup

In the field of environmental cleanup, nanomaterials are crucial. You can modify them to clean up polluted environments like the air, water, and ground. Due to their high surface area and reactivity, they can be used in a wide variety of environmental remediation applications.

Industrial and municipal effluents have been treated with nanomaterials, such as nanoparticles and nanocomposites, to degrade hazardous organic compounds and remove heavy metals. Nanoscale catalysts are also used in environmental remediation to speed up the breakdown of harmful chemicals and pollutants, helping to lessen the overall impact of human activities on the environment.

The Tenth Improvement in Drug Delivery

The use of nanomaterials in medicine delivery has resulted in a dramatically improved, more precise method of administering medication. Nanomaterial-based drug delivery systems are able to encapsulate medications, transport them to targeted areas in the body, and then gradually release the drugs for prolonged therapeutic benefits.

Drugs are typically delivered by liposomes, polymer nanoparticles, or lipid-based nanoparticles. Controlled-release formulations improve drug solubility and stability, allowing for less frequent dosage and fewer adverse effects. Drugs can be delivered to areas that conventional drug delivery systems can't reach, such the brain, thanks to nanoparticles' ability to cross biological barriers like the blood-brain barrier.

Effective Methods for Storing and Transforming Energy
Nanomaterials have made important advances in energy storage and conversion.

# Chapter 3.
# Use of Nanotechnology in Healthcare

## 3.1- Nanomedicine and its impact on

The Role of Nanotechnology in Healthcare

The revolutionary field of nanomedicine, which lies at the crossroads of nanotechnology and medicine, is dramatically altering the healthcare system as we know it. Diseases are identified, treated, and avoided with the help of nanomaterials, nanodevices, and nanotechniques. Nanomaterials' unusual features, their molecular-level interaction with biological systems, and their focused delivery techniques have created promising new avenues for medical research and practise. This article delves into the revolutionary effects of nanomedicine on the medical field.

One, Precisely Aiming Drugs to Patients

Targeted medication delivery is one of nanomedicine's most exciting and consequential uses. Systemic delivery, the kind used in conventional medication administration, has been linked to adverse reactions, poor drug dispersion, and even harm to healthy organs. By allowing for targeted drug delivery to specific cells and tissues, nanomedicine provides a solution to these problems.

Liposomes and polymeric nanoparticles are two types of nanoparticles that can be modified to encapsulate medications and deliver them selectively to sick cells. This pinpoint accuracy lessens adverse reactions and maximises the drug's therapeutic benefit. For use in cancer therapy, for instance, chemotherapeutic medicines carried onto nanocarriers can be delivered selectively to tumour cells while sparing normal tissues. Treatment success is increased, and the patient's quality of life is enhanced, thanks to this tailored drug delivery method.

2. Individualised Health Care

Nanomedicine is a major force in personalised medicine, which takes into account a patient's unique genetic makeup, lifestyle, and other characteristics when developing an individualised treatment plan. With personalised medicine, doctors may tailor their recommendations for therapy to each individual patient, ensuring the best possible outcomes with minimal side effects.

To a large extent, nanotechnology is responsible for this shift in perspective. Molecular diagnostics based on nanoparticles functionalized with specific biomolecules are currently in development. This data aids medical practitioners in making informed treatment decisions. Nanocarriers can also carry unique combinations of drugs, allowing for better treatment for each individual.

(3) Improved Diagnostic Imaging

Thanks to innovations in nanomedicine, medical imaging has come a long way. Improvements in the sensitivity, specificity, and resolution of imaging modalities like MRI, CT scans, and PET scans have been achieved through the use of nanoparticles and nanoscale contrast ants.

To better visualise certain tissues or organs, magnetic nanoparticles can be utilised as contrast agents in magnetic resonance imaging (MRI). Semiconductor quantum dots have found use in spectrally accurate fields such as molecular imaging and diagnostics. Thanks to these developments, doctors and nurses now have access to more complete data for disease diagnosis and tracking.

4 Early Detection of Disease

The key to effective therapy and better patient outcomes is oftentimes early disease identification. New methods for spotting diseases at their most curable stages have been made possible by nanomedicine. Disease indicators or antigens can be targeted by functionalizing nanoparticles with specific biomolecules.

Tiny levels of biomarkers in blood or other body fluids can be detected using nanoscale sensors and contrast agents, allowing for early detection of cancer. These nanosensors can also measure temporal changes in disease indicators, allowing for better disease progression monitoring and tailored treatment.

Five. Renewal Medical Practises

Regenerative medicine, which aims to repair dysfunctional or diseased bodily structures, has benefited greatly from the application of nanotechnology. Scaffolds that imitate the natural extracellular matrix and assist tissue growth are made using nanomaterials like nanofibers and nanoparticles.

Nanofibrous scaffolds, for instance, have been shown to aid in the repair of a variety of tissues, including skin, bone, and cartilage. These scaffolds are able to promote tissue growth, repair, and regeneration because they have a nanoscale structure similar to that of the patient's own tissue. The incorporation of nanoparticles into these scaffolds can improve their capabilities, such as the delivery of drugs in a regulated fashion to speed up the healing process.

Nanodiagnostics, number six

The subject of nanotherapeutics and nanodiagnostics is rapidly developing. The process entails creating nanoparticles with dual diagnostic and therapeutic capabilities. Because of the diagnostic and therapeutic capabilities built into these nanoparticles, the process of diagnosing and treating disease is streamlined.
Multifunctional nanoparticles used in cancer therapy are an example of nanotheranostics. These nanoparticles have the ability to image

for the presence of tumours, transport therapeutic chemicals to the tumour location, and track the effectiveness of the treatment. This holistic method streamlines disease care and cuts down on redundant treatments.

## 7. Enhanced Vaccine Distribution

Vaccines could be administered with greater efficacy and greater patient compliance with the use of nanotechnology. Nanovaccines have the potential to generate more powerful and long-lasting immune responses than traditional vaccinations, which may require numerous doses to acquire protection.

By encapsulating antigens and delivering them to immune cells in a more targeted manner, vaccinations based on nanoparticles can improve immune responses. They also permit regulated release, which maintains antigen presentation and immune activation throughout time. This method has great potential for the creation of vaccinations against cancer and infectious disorders.

## Breaking the Blood-Brain Barrier, Number 8.

The blood-brain barrier (BBB) is a protective barrier that restricts the entry of chemicals into the brain via the circulatory system. Nanoparticles that can traverse the BBB and deliver medications to the brain are being developed as part of an effort to overcome this obstacle in nanomedicine.

Liposomes and dendrimers are two types of nanoparticles that can be manipulated to transport medications over the BBB without compromising their effectiveness. The capacity to do so expands the range of options for treating neurological conditions like neurodegenerative illnesses and brain tumours.

## Minimally Invasive Methods, Number Nine

Thanks to advancements in nanomedicine, less invasive surgical options are now available, allowing doctors to minimise discomfort, downtime, and scarring for their patients. The human body is incredibly complex, but nanoscale devices can be engineered to navigate it with pinpoint accuracy.

Nanorobots, for instance, are being created for use in minimally invasive surgeries and the delivery of drugs to specific areas. These microrobots are able to navigate the circulatory system, identify infected cells, and precisely deposit their therapeutic payloads. The need for invasive procedures is mitigated since they can be directed to particular locations inside the body.Tenth, Efforts to Reduce Antibiotic ResistanceThe spread of germs resistant to antibiotics is a major health risk around the world. The creation of nanoparticles with antibacterial characteristics is one way in which nanotechnology may help with this issue.

For instance, silver nanoparticles have been used into wound dressings, medical equipment, and textiles due to their demonstrated antibacterial action. Antibiotics' efficacy against drug-resistant bacteria can be further improved by employing nanomaterials to improve their distribution.Chronic Diseases and Their Treatment

Managing and monitoring patients with chronic diseases like diabetes and cardiovascular disease can be a full-time job. As a result of advancements in nanomedicine, implanted nanosensors and drug delivery systems are now available.

Nanosensors implanted under the skin can monitor glucose levels in the blood and prompt the body to secrete insulin as needed, making them a promising tool in the control of diabetes. This closed-loop technology provides accurate regulation of blood sugar and lessens the likelihood of hypoglycemia. Other chronic diseases can be treated with similarly constructed systems.

## 3.2- Nanoscale drug delivery and diagnostics

Drug delivery and diagnosis at the nanoscale

One of the most exciting applications of nanotechnology in medicine is the development of nanoscale medication delivery and diagnostics. Nanomedicine is an emerging discipline that uses nanomaterials and nanodevices to improve illness diagnosis and treatment. Researchers and medical professionals are making great achievements in patient care, lowered side effects, and improved treatment outcomes by utilising nanoscale technologies. The effects of nanotechnology on medicine and medicine's ability to diagnose disease are explored here.

1.Nanoscale diagnostics for precision medicine

The cornerstone of successful medical treatment is the correct and timely diagnosis of diseases. Diseases may be detected with unprecedented sensitivity and specificity using nanoscale diagnostics. With their help, we can now develop personalised and targeted treatment plans by identifying specific molecular markers or biomolecules associated with certain diseases. Some essential features of diagnostics at the nanoscale include:

a. Premature Disease Diagnosis:
   Molecularly early disease detection is made possible by nanoscale diagnostic tools like nanoparticles functionalized with disease-specific biomarkers. This can greatly boost a patient's chances of a successful treatment and better outcomes. Small levels of tumor-specific biomarkers in blood or other biological fluids, for instance, can be detected by nanosensors long before any noticeable symptoms of cancer manifest.

c. Testing Done Right At The Point Of Care:

Point-of-care testing with nanoscale diagnostic devices paves the way for immediate, on-site disease diagnosis. These portable or hand-held devices are invaluable in times of crisis, in uncharted territory, or when every second counts. Thanks to advancements in nanotechnology, portable and simple medical testing equipment is now a reality.

Biomarker Profiling (subheading c)
   Nanotechnology in diagnostics has made it possible to profile several different biomarkers at once. This can help doctors develop a more complete picture of the patient's condition, which can lead to better treatment choices. Diseases with complicated aetiologies, like cardiovascular disease, can benefit greatly from the ability to analyse a large number of biomarkers.

Nanoparticles as a Possible Method of Drug Delivery

The distribution and administration of drugs within the body have been greatly improved by nanoscale drug delivery devices. The utilisation of nanoparticles for targeted drug delivery is central to these systems. There are many benefits to using this method of targeted medicine delivery instead of the standard method.

a. Specific Administration of Drugs:
   Targeting medications to specific cells or tissues is one of the main benefits of nanoscale drug delivery. Liposomes and polymeric nanoparticles can be modified so that they only bind to and attach to sick cells. This specific method reduces the drug's adverse effects and boosts its beneficial ones.

Enhanced drug solubility (b)
   Some medications aren't easily dissolved in water, which might make dosing and administration more complicated. It is possible to encapsulate these medications in nanoparticles and increase their

bioavailability. This not only improves the efficiency of drug delivery, but also raises the drug's bioavailability.

b. Prolonged Dose Administration:
   Drugs can be released slowly over time from nanoparticles thanks to careful engineering. The continuous therapeutic impact and decreased dose frequency are the results of the sustained release mechanism. This method is especially helpful for treating chronic diseases over the course of treatment.

3. Liposomes as a Method of Drug Delivery

The medical community has recently become increasingly interested in liposomes, a specific form of nanoscale drug delivery mechanism. They can enclose several different medications in their lipid bilayer exterior and water within. This is the impact liposomes are having:

a. Cancer Therapy:
   In the fight against cancer, liposomal medication delivery has proven to be an effective strategy. It is possible to load chemotherapy drugs onto liposomes and direct them to tumour cells. This pinpoint accuracy improves chemotherapy's efficacy while decreasing its negative effects on healthy tissues.

b) Transport of Drugs to the Brain:
   The blood-brain barrier (BBB) is a selective transport barrier between the blood and the brain. Drugs can be delivered to the brain via liposomes that have been modified to pass across the BBB. This skill can be used to treat brain tumours and other illnesses that affect the central nervous system in novel ways.

Nanorobotic Drug Delivery Systems (4)

Nanorobots, often known as nanobots, are an exciting new frontier in the field of medicine delivery. Nanobots are miniaturised devices engineered to successfully navigate the human body. They have extraordinary accuracy in their ability to navigate the circulatory system, target specific cells or tissues, and release therapeutic payloads. Here are some of the ways in which nanorobots will change the face of medicine:

a. Specific Intervention:
   Nanorobots could one day be used to administer precise medical care. Drugs can be delivered directly to the site of disease thanks to their ability to identify and bind to sick cells. The precision helps lessen the risk of unwanted effects while increasing the therapeutic benefit.

b) Minimally Invasive Methods:
   Nanorobots have the potential to make less invasive surgical procedures routine. These miniaturised devices can be precisely directed to their surgical targets, reducing the likelihood of unintended tissue damage and other complications.

b. Medication Administration Control:
   Nanorobots can be programmed to dispense medication on demand or at set intervals. The therapeutic impact can be precisely timed and managed thanks to the controlled release system.

The Role of Nanotechnology in Drug Delivery, Part 5

An emerging discipline, nanotherapeutics integrates diagnosis and treatment into a unified framework. The process entails creating nanoparticles with dual diagnostic and therapeutic capabilities. These multipurpose nanoparticles may one day make illness management easier by:

a. Diagnosis and Treatment of Illness:
   Nanoparticles with many uses can be used to image for illness detection, deliver therapeutic drugs to the site of the disease, and

track the effectiveness of the treatment. This holistic method streamlines disease care and cuts down on redundant treatments.

b Real-time Observation:

Nanoparticles used in nanodiagnostics can report on the status of a condition and how well a treatment is working in near-real time. Incorporating this data into the treatment process at the right moments is crucial.

b. Tailored Care: Nanotheranostics facilitates individualised treatment plans. The diagnostic function can zero in on discrete illness signs or traits, allowing for the application of individualised treatments.

6. Improved Brain Drug DeliveryThe blood-brain barrier (BBB) is a protective barrier that inhibits the entry of chemicals from the bloodstream into the brain, which can slow down the delivery of medications to the brain. The field of nanomedicine is working to overcome this obstacle by creating nanomaterials with the ability to penetrate the BBB and deliver therapeutics to the brain.

a. Brain-Delivered Nanoparticles:

Liposomes and dendrimers are two types of nanoparticles that can be manipulated to transport medications over the BBB without compromising their effectiveness. The capacity to do so expands the range of options for treating neurological conditions like neurodegenerative illnesses and brain tumours.

b. Neurodegenerative Diseases and Alzheimer's:

In the fight against neurodegenerative illnesses like Alzheimer's, the capacity to transport medications directly to the brain is crucial. Therapeutic compounds that delay the disease's course and boost cognitive function are being researched, and their possible delivery on nanoparticles is being investigated.Seventhly, Efforts to Reduce Antibiotic Resistance

# Chapter 4.
# Electronics and Nanotechnology

## 4.1- Miniaturization and advances in electronics

Reduced size and technological progress in electronics.

The idea of miniaturisation has been crucial in propelling the field of electronics forward at a breakneck pace during the past few decades. As technology has shrunk in size, it has also grown in strength, efficiency, and pervasiveness in our daily lives. From microchips and sensors to wearable technology and the Internet of Things (IoT), this article examines the significance of miniaturisation and its tremendous impact on the area of electronics.

The First Stages of Miniaturisation

Miniaturisation is the reduction in size of electronic components and devices without a corresponding decrease in functionality. This idea has been crucial throughout the development of electronics, allowing for smaller and more powerful devices to be created. Several major breakthroughs can be used to reconstruct the history of miniaturisation:

Transistors and ICs, first. The transistor's introduction to electronics in the middle of the 20th century was a watershed moment. By using semiconductors instead of cumbersome vacuum tubes, the size of electronic devices was greatly reduced. Because of this change, microchips, also known as integrated circuits (ICs), are now possible. The advent of microchips ushered in a new era of computers and digitised society.

(a) Moore's Law Gordon Moore, co-founder of Intel, first noticed that the number of transistors on a microchip quadrupled roughly every two years, and he named this phenomenon Moore's Law. For decades, this notion has served as the foundation for the steady reduction in size and increase in efficiency of electronic equipment. It's what's allowing computing power to increase at an exponential rate.

Microelectromechanical (MEMS) systems c. MEMS refers to microelectromechanical systems that are created on semiconductor chips. They have several uses, from sensors to accelerometers and gyroscopes. Miniaturised Electromechanical Systems (MEMS) technology has allowed for the creation of portable electronics like smartphones and game controllers.

Dissertation on Nanoelectronics: Nanoelectronics is a subfield of electronics that further reduces the size of components by working with structures on a nanoscale scale. Researchers are working to perfect nanoscale transistors and other components so that electronic gadgets can continue to get smaller, faster, and more efficient.

Effects on Computing (2)

The computing industry has been revolutionised by miniaturisation. Processors are now faster and more efficient than ever thanks to the miniaturisation of transistors and microchips. As a result, this has fuelled development in several areas of computing:

Processing Time Reduction (a) More calculations can be done in less time since more transistors can fit on a device thanks to miniaturisation. As a result, computing speeds have increased dramatically, making today's computers far more powerful than their forebears.

b. Efficient Use of Energy: Reduced power consumption is another benefit of miniaturising transistors. This is especially important for mobile computing, where saving power is a top priority.

Enhanced Capacity to Remember Information (c) Solid-state drives (SSDs) and random access memory (RAM) are two examples of high-capacity memory modules made possible by miniaturisation, both of which store and retrieve data quickly. The overall efficiency of the system has been vastly enhanced by this.

Reduced Physical Size (d) As a result of miniaturisation, a wide variety of handheld and wearable computer devices have emerged. These gadgets not only make life easier, but they also provide exciting new opportunities for independence and accessibility.

Thirdly, the IoT (Internet of Things).

A network of interconnected devices and items that can collect and share data is what the term Internet of Things (IoT) refers to. In example, the miniaturisation of sensors and microcontrollers has allowed for the development of the IoT. Here's how miniaturisation aids in the expansion of the Internet of Things:

a. Miniaturising Sensors Everyday items, appliances, and industrial machinery can now incorporate miniaturised sensors like accelerometers, temperature sensors, and humidity sensors. These sensors gather information, which is then sent to other gadgets or the cloud.

b. Small Microcontrollers: The computing power needed by IoT devices is provided by miniaturised microcontrollers such as single-board computers like the Raspberry Pi. These gadgets are perfect for a variety of uses because of their compact size, low power consumption, and low cost.

Clothing-integrated electronics (c) Wearable technologies like smartwatches and fitness trackers are the result of the miniaturisation of electronics. These gadgets connect to mobile devices and the Internet of Things (IoT) ecosystem to collect data on the user's health, fitness, and other metrics.

## 4. Medical Technology

Medical equipment design, patient care, and hospital workflow have all been profoundly influenced by miniaturisation. Notable effects can be shown in several domains:

a. Mobile Health Equipment There are now handheld ultrasound units, blood glucose monitors, and even small magnetic resonance imaging scanners thanks to miniaturisation. These tools are easier to obtain, which expedites the time it takes to detect a problem and cure it.

The miniaturisation of implantable devices including pacemakers, neural stimulators, and drug delivery systems has allowed for less intrusive treatments to address a wide range of medical diseases. Minimally invasive procedures can be used to insert these devices, minimising trauma to the patient and the duration of their recuperation.

Connected Health Trackers (c) Long-term use of wearable health equipment like heart rate monitors and continuous glucose monitoring does not have to compromise on discretion or comfort. They facilitate preventative health monitoring by individuals and enable the transmission of data to medical professionals for remote monitoring.

## Fifthly, Electronics and Nanotechnology

Miniaturisation of electronics has been greatly aided by nanotechnology, the engineering and manipulation of materials at the nanoscale. The electrical, thermal, and mechanical properties of nanomaterials like carbon nanotubes and graphene are unprecedented. Nanotechnology's impact on electronics can be summarised as follows:a. Transistors at the Nanoscale Using nanomaterials like carbon nanotubes and nanowires, scientists are investigating the potential of tiny transistors. In the future, these nanoscale transistors may take the place of more common silicon transistors, furthering the miniaturisation trend.

Storage Devices at the Nanoscale b. Resistive random-access memory (RRAM) and phase-change memory (PCM) are two examples of non-volatile memory devices being researched with nanoscale materials. The data density and transfer rates of these devices are superior.

c. Sensors on a Nanoscale: Environmental monitoring and medical diagnostics are only two examples of the many fields that can benefit from the very sensitive and selective sensors made possible by nanotechnology. Most of the time, these nanoscale sensors are more dependable, efficient, and compact than their macroscale equivalents.Sustainability and energy efficiency

One of the goals of miniaturisation in electronics is to reduce power consumption without sacrificing functionality. In general, the power consumption of smaller components is lower. Several aspects of sustainability are affected by this energy efficiency:

a. Decreased Need for Electrical Power: Electronics that are more energy efficient use less electricity, which in turn lowers their carbon impact. This is of utmost importance for apps that run on mobile devices, IoT sensors, and use batteries.Energy-efficient devices can help reduce greenhouse gas emissions and electronic waste, both of which have a positive effect on the environment. As technology improves, its effect on the environment grows smaller.

Longer battery life is a common feature of smaller, more efficient devices, which can be very helpful when travelling.

## 4.2- Nanoelectronics and quantum computing

Nanotechnology and quantum computing represent cutting-edge developments in electronics.

Nanoelectronics and quantum computing are at the vanguard of a technological revolution that is about to sweep the electronics industry. Our understanding of computing, memory, and information processing is being revolutionised by these cutting-edge disciplines. In this essay, we delve into the exciting field of nanoelectronics and quantum computing, discussing its history, current state of development, and potential future applications.

One: Miniaturising Electronics using Nanotechnology

Nanoelectronics is the study and creation of electrical devices and components on the nanoscale scale. It expands upon the principle of miniaturisation by shrinking electronic parts to infinitesimally small sizes. As technology shrinks, it becomes more powerful, faster, and more adaptable. Some fundamental features of nanoelectronics are as follows:

a. Measured in Nanometers: Structures and components in nanoelectronics are typically one billionth of a metre in size. Changes in material properties at this size provide up novel avenues for electronic design.

B. Beyond Transistors: The transistor is a crucial component in virtually all current electronic systems. Smaller and more efficient transistors have allowed for the development of more potent and less energy-hungry electronic gadgets as miniaturisation has progressed.

c Progress in the Field of Materials Science: Nanoelectronics rely on cutting-edge materials with exceptional electrical and thermal properties, such as carbon nanotubes and graphene. Researchers are looking at these substances to see if they may be used in place of silicon in electronics.

d) Outside the Silicon World: While silicon has served as the electronic industry's backbone for decades, as the field continues to shrink, researchers are exploring alternatives. Nanoelectronics is expanding beyond silicon as scientists investigate the potential of organic materials, two-dimensional materials, and even quantum dots.

Using Quantum Mechanics in Computing (Second)

Quantum computing is an emerging topic that uses quantum physics to provide novel approaches to computational problem solving. Quantum computers, in contrast to classical computers, use quantum bits, also known as qubits, to process data. When applied to issues that are now too difficult for classical computers, quantum computing has the potential to radically alter the computing landscape. Some fundamentals of quantum computing are as follows:

Superposition with Qubits (a) The two possible values for a classical bit are 0 and 1. However, due to a phenomenon known as superposition, qubits can concurrently occupy more than one state. This paves the way for quantum computers to test numerous hypotheses simultaneously.

In terms of (b) Quantum Entanglement: The state of one qubit can get entangled with the state of another, even if the two qubits are separated in space. Because of this quality, quantum computers may now efficiently conduct extremely complicated computations.

b. Increasing Velocity Exponentially: Some issues, such as those in cryptography, optimisation, and materials research, may be solved exponentially faster on a quantum computer. They can accomplish in seconds what would take traditional computers generations to accomplish.

As for d. Quantum Algorithms: Researchers are working on quantum algorithms to take use of quantum computers' peculiar strengths. For instance, Shor's technique may factor big numbers at an exponential rate quicker than classical algorithms, which could compromise existing encryption protocols.

Nanoelectronics and quantum computing: a meeting of the minds

The future of electronics and data processing will be shaped in large part by the intersection of nanoelectronics and quantum computing. See how they overlap below:

a. Qubits Based on Quantum Dots Physical mechanisms such as superconducting circuits, trapped ions, and topological qubits are all viable options for realising qubits in quantum computing. Quantum dots, which are tiny semiconductor structures, are currently being investigated as a potential source for qubits. Due to their tunable qubit characteristics, quantum dots are an attractive technology for quantum computing.

b. Fabrication of Quantum Hardware: Qubits and quantum gates are two examples of quantum hardware, and nanoscale methods are frequently used in their manufacture. The exact structures required for quantum computing can only be made with the help of nanofabrication techniques. Therefore, developments in nanoelectronics are essential to the realisation of hardware for quantum computing.

d. The Role of Quantum Dots in Conventional Electronics Nanoelectronics' usage of quantum dots has showed promise for application in more traditional electronic gadgets. They can be used in quantum dot-based lasers, memory devices, and transistors. The complementary nature of nanoelectronics and quantum dots is highlighted by this overlap.

d. Quantum Hardware Based on Nanoscale Transistors: Supporting the management and measurement of qubits in quantum computers relies heavily on the development of nanoscale transistors and electrical components. In order to build the control electronics required for quantum systems, high-performance transistors are required.

4. The Promise and Peril of Quantum Computing

While quantum computing has much potential, it also has many obstacles to overcome.

Decoherence in Quantum Systems, a. A process known as quantum decoherence occurs when a quantum system is perturbed by something from the outside world. Since qubits' quantum states are fragile, this can reduce the amount of time they can spend computing before mistakes occur. Scientists are actively developing mistake correcting methods to address this problem.

Expandability (b) The development of reliable, large-scale quantum computers is still a difficult task. We are currently in the NISQ (noisy intermediate-scale quantum) age of quantum computing, which is characterised by low qubit counts and high mistake rates.

3. c Quantum Algorithms: There is persistent effort to create quantum algorithms that can outperform classical algorithms in a variety of real-world scenarios. There is a wide gap between the maturity of some quantum algorithms and their early days.

d. Quantum Encryption: Threatening current security measures is the possibility that quantum computers could crack popular forms of encryption. However, quantum cryptography provides options for ensuring private communication by utilising quantum mechanics' peculiarities.

## 5. Quantum Computing's Practical Uses

The ability of quantum computers to efficiently tackle complicated problems has the potential to cause a revolution in many different areas. Some examples of popular uses are as follows:

Cryptography (a) Current encryption systems may be vulnerable to quantum computers since they can factor huge numbers exponentially quicker than classical computers. The goal of post-quantum cryptography is to create encryption methods impenetrable by quantum computers.

b Drug Development: The accuracy of quantum computer simulations of molecular interactions is unprecedented. By modelling molecular behaviour and anticipating interactions with possible drug candidates, this expertise speeds up the drug discovery process.

Optimisation Issues (c): Optimisation issues including routing, scheduling, and resource allocation are ideal applications for quantum computing. Quantum algorithms have the potential to expedite the discovery of optimal solutions to such difficult issues.

Science of Materials (d) By simulating their quantum behaviour, quantum computers help scientists create novel materials tailored to specific needs. This can be used for energy storage, electronics, and materials research.

e. A.I. : artificial intelligence Machine learning algorithms may benefit from the speedups offered by quantum computing in areas like pattern identification and optimisation. Emerging research in quantum machine learning brings together quantum computers and artificial intelligence.

Nanoelectronics and Computing's Future

The field of computing and information processing is undergoing radical change as a result of nanoelectronics. As

# Chapter 5.
# Energy and Nanotechnology

## 5.1- Nanomaterials for renewable energy sources

The Impact of Nanomaterials on Renewable Energy and Sustainability.

To combat climate change, depleting fossil fuel supplies, and rising energy demands, the search for renewable energy sources has gone global. Nanomaterials are quickly becoming a game-changer in the search for environmentally friendly energy sources. Improvements in renewable energy technology can be directly attributed to their distinctive nanoscale features, such as enhanced surface area and catalytic activity. In this essay, we discuss the essential function of nanomaterials in the generation, transmission, and storage of clean energy.

1. Nanomaterials for Solar Energy Collection

Solar energy is one of the cleanest and most plentiful renewable energy sources, and significant advances in solar cell technology have been made because to nanomaterials.

a. Greater Productivity: Quantum dots and perovskite materials, two types of nanomaterials, have been incorporated into solar cells to improve their ability to absorb light and to separate electrons and holes. Because of this improvement, more electricity can now be generated from the same quantity of sunshine.

In terms of b. Thin-Film Solar Cells: Thin-film solar cells, which are both portable and adaptable, are made possible by nanomaterials. Making solar energy more widely available, these cells can be incorporated into a variety of surfaces, from buildings to portable electronic devices.

b) Solar cells that are see-through Windows, glass facades, and other transparent surfaces can have nanomaterial-built transparent solar cells put to them to generate electricity without blocking the view. They collect sunlight while letting through visible light.

d) Solar cells made from perovskite Due to their high efficiency and low production costs, solar cells based on perovskites have received a lot of interest. The exceptional performance of these cells can be attributed in part to the utilisation of nanoscale perovskite materials.

The Role of Nanomaterials in Wind Power

Nanomaterials have made great progress in boosting the efficiency of wind turbines, making wind energy a more significant part of the renewable energy landscape.

a. Materials That Don't Weigh You Down: Carbon nanotube and graphene-based nanocomposites can be used to make stronger and more lightweight wind turbine blades. Blade weight is decreased while structural integrity is preserved thanks to the use of these materials.

Enhanced Aerodynamics, (b) Blades on wind turbines can benefit from nanocoatings that improve their aerodynamics, leading to less resistance and a higher rate of energy conversion. Air turbulence can be mitigated by using nanostructured surfaces to direct the flow of air.

c High-Tech Sensors: The efficiency and durability of wind turbine parts may be tracked in real time by nanosensors. Maintenance requirements can be anticipated, and catastrophic failures avoided, with the use of this technology.

The Role of Nanomaterials in Battery Technology

Integrating variable renewable energy sources into the system relies heavily on efficient energy storage. The development of energy storage technology is greatly aided by nanomaterials:

The a. Lithium-Ion Battery Incorporating nanomaterials like nanostructured anodes and cathodes into lithium-ion batteries has greatly increased their energy density and cycle life. As a result of these developments, batteries used in things like electric vehicles and consumer devices are now more powerful and can endure for longer periods of time.

Supercapacitors, b. Electrostatic energy is stored in supercapacitors, also called ultracapacitors. By increasing their capacitance and energy density, nanomaterials in supercapacitors have made them useful for fast energy storage and release.

The c. Sodium-Ion Battery An emerging substitute for lithium-ion batteries is sodium-ion batteries. High-performance sodium-ion battery electrodes have been developed with the use of nanomaterials; these electrodes can be less expensive and more numerous than their lithium equivalents.

d) Materials with a high energy density: The feasibility of storing hydrogen in nanomaterials for later use in fuel cells is being investigated. Clean hydrogen energy production and storage could benefit from hydrogen storage materials with high surface areas and improved adsorption characteristics.

(4) Hydrogen Production Using Nanomaterials

Hydrogen has the potential to be used in fuel cells and transportation because it is a clean fuel. The use of nanomaterials in the generation and storage of hydrogen is important.
As for a. photocatalysis: Nanomaterials, and semiconductor nanoparticles in particular, have found utility as photocatalysts for

the solar-powered electrolysis of water. Photocatalytic water splitting is a technique that could be used to generate clean hydrogen fuel.

b. Hydrogen Energy Storage: Hydrogen storage can be improved with the help of nanomaterials, which include large surface areas and can be engineered to have certain adsorption characteristics. Hydrogen storage in these materials is made possible by the reduced pressures and temperatures required.

Catalysts for use in fuel cells (c) Hydrogen and oxygen react electrochemically in fuel cells, producing electricity. Platinum nanoparticles and other nanomaterials are utilised as catalysts to speed up this reaction and boost the efficiency and longevity of fuel cells.

5. The Use of Nanotechnology in Making Biofuels

Biodiesel and bioethanol are two examples of biofuels; both are produced from organic matter like plants or algae. Improved methods for creating biofuels with the use of nanomaterials are currently in the works.

a. Biofuels from algae: Algae can be grown and harvested more efficiently using nanomaterials, which is useful for making biofuel. Algal growth can be enhanced by nanoparticles in three ways: nutrition delivery, light absorption, and $CO_2$ uptake.

Catalysis, b. The production of biofuels from biomass feedstocks requires the employment of nanocatalysts. They speed up the chemical processes needed to make bioethanol and biodiesel, requiring less effort and time to complete the transformation.

c. Coatings Made From Nanomaterials: Equipment used in the manufacture of biofuels can have its lifespan increased by applying nanomaterial coatings, which also serve to protect the machinery from corrosion and fouling.

Geothermal and tidal energy 6. Nanomaterials

Even though geothermal and tidal energy are stable and consistent, they need specialised materials to be fully utilised.

Superior Heat Exchangers, a. Nanomaterial coatings on heat exchangers can increase heat transfer rates and decrease fouling, leading to greater efficiency in geothermal energy.

b. Blades of Tidal Turbines Tidal turbine blades can be strengthened using nanomaterials like carbon nanotubes, making them more resilient and resistant to corrosion in saltwater.

7. Obstacles and Future Steps

Despite nanoparticles' promising future in renewable energy, several obstacles and research avenues remain.

Expandability (a) Many nanomaterials are made in very small quantities in labs. In order to address the needs of large-scale energy applications, production must be scaled up, which is still a hurdle.

b Repercussions on the Environment: Nanomaterial manufacturing and disposal can have negative effects on the natural world. It is critical to study the environmental effects and conduct a lifecycle analysis of these materials.

b) Efficacy in Relation to Price: In order to compete with traditional energy sources in the marketplace, renewable energy technology must be affordable. Nanomaterial synthesis and integration research must continue at a reasonable cost.

d) Security: Nanomaterials' use in energy applications necessitates a careful evaluation of the concerns they may pose to human health.

To guarantee uniformity and quality in renewable energy technologies, it is necessary to standardise nanomaterial production and characterization processes.

f Cross-Disciplinary Work: Collaboration between material scientists, engineers, and energy experts is essential for progress in nanomaterials research for renewable energy. Complex problems in need of multidisciplinary study and collaboration.

## 5.2- Nanotech solutions for energy storage and conversion

Energy storage and conversion using nanotechnology.

Today, the urgent need for renewable energy has sparked a global energy revolution. Materials and gadgets that can be manipulated at the nanoscale, thanks to nanotechnology, are at the vanguard of this revolution. It provides novel approaches to energy storage and conversion with the potential to revolutionise the generation, distribution, and use of power. In this article, we delve into the fascinating world of nanotech energy storage and conversion options, including state-of-the-art battery technology and solar cells.

One Use for Nanomaterials: Energy Storage

Incorporating Nanomaterials into Lithium-Ion Batteries: Smartphones and electric cars are just two of the many technologies that rely on lithium-ion batteries. The use of nanomaterials like graphene and silicon nanoparticles has improved the efficiency of these batteries.

(2) Extremely High Energy Density: Anodes made of nanoscale silicon can significantly boost power density. Silicon has a larger capacity for absorbing and releasing lithium ions, leading to longer-lasting, more powerful batteries.

c. Increased Stability of the Electrode Nanomaterial coatings, such as graphene or carbon nanotubes, can improve electrode durability and delay electrode degradation.

Reduced Charging Time for Electric Vehicles and Portable Devices (d) Nanoscale anode materials can enable faster charging and discharging.

f. Moving Past Lithium-Ion: Next-generation batteries, such as lithium-sulfur and solid-state batteries, provide even more energy storage potential and are being investigated for application with nanomaterials.

## (2) Nanotechnology-Based Improvements in Supercapacitors

Ultracapacitors, or supercapacitors, are a type of energy storage device that uses the surface of electrodes to hold electrical charge. They are perfect for uses that call for a lot of power, as they can store and release that power quickly.

a. Electrodes Made of Nanomaterials: Nanomaterials used as electrodes in supercapacitors have many advantages. Carbon nanotubes, graphene, and metal oxides are examples of high-surface-area materials that can improve energy storage and power density.

b. Increased Energy Storage due to Greater Capacitance achieved by Nanomaterial-Based Supercapacitors.

c. Quick Recharge: Applications where fast energy release is required, such as regenerative braking in electric vehicles, benefit greatly from the rapid charging and discharging capabilities of supercapacitors with electrodes made of nanomaterials.

## 3. Nanotechnology-Based Strategies for Converting Solar Energy

Nanotechnology is revolutionising the efficiency and adaptability of solar cells, making use of this renewable and abundant energy source.

The a. Thin-Film Solar Cell Thin-film solar cells can be easily integrated into a variety of surfaces, from buildings to portable electronic gadgets, due to their small size, low weight, and pliability. In order to make thin-film solar cells, nanomaterials like cadmium telluride and perovskite are employed.

b. Enhanced Productivity: Improved energy conversion efficiency is achieved by using nanomaterials to increase solar cells' capacity to absorb light. For instance, quantum dots can be integrated into solar cells to absorb a wider range of the sun's radiation.

b) Solar cells that are see-through Windows and other transparent surfaces can have nanomaterial-made transparent solar cells adhered to them to harvest sunlight without impeding the view.

d) Solar cells made from perovskite Nanoscale perovskite materials have helped boost the impressive efficiency of perovskite solar cells. The great efficiency and low production costs of these cells make them a promising technology for solar power.

Hydrogen production using nanomaterials

Hydrogen is widely regarded as a clean and flexible energy source. It can be made in a number of ways, one of which is by splitting water with nanomaterials.

a. Hydrogen Production by Photocatalysis: When exposed to light, nanomaterials, and more specifically semiconductor nanoparticles, can catalyse the splitting of water molecules. These materials can be used to generate hydrogen fuel from water using only the power of the sun.

Catalysts Based on Nanomaterials, b. Platinum nanoparticles and other nanomaterials are utilised as catalysts in the synthesis of hydrogen from natural gas and other sources. These catalysts make hydrogen production more efficient.

Improvements in Hydrogen Storage (c) Hydrogen storage enhancement by nanomaterials is another area of research. Hydrogen can be stored at lower pressures and temperatures using materials with high surface areas and customised adsorption characteristics.

## Nanomaterials for Fuel Cells, No. 5

Electrochemical devices called fuel cells may transform the chemical energy of a fuel like hydrogen into electricity. There are a number of ways in which nanomaterials are improving fuel cell technology.

a. Fuel Cell Catalysts: Nanoparticles of precious metals like platinum and palladium serve as catalysts in fuel cells. They make fuel cells more efficient and long-lasting by boosting the pace at which electrochemical processes take place.

b. PEMs (Proton-Exchange Membranes): Nanomaterials enhance the mechanical strength and proton conductivity of proton exchange membranes in fuel cells. The fuel cell's total efficiency is improved because to these upgrades.

Fuel cells that directly use methanol (type c): The use of nanomaterials in direct methanol fuel cells, which can produce electricity from methanol, is currently under investigation. These cells could be used to power mobile devices.

## Conversion of Thermoelectric Energy Using Nanomaterials 6

Thermoelectric materials are special because they can change one form of energy into another. The effectiveness of thermoelectric devices has been greatly enhanced by the use of nanomaterials:

Improved Thermoelectric Performance, a. In order to make extremely effective thermoelectric materials, scientists have designed nanomaterials with low heat conductivity and high electrical conductivity. Thermoelectric generators use these materials to transform thermal energy into electrical energy.

Thermoelectrics that can bend and stretch Wearable electronics, sensor networks, and other uses that rely on energy harvesting can all benefit from thermoelectric devices made from nanomaterials.

Smart Grid Energy Storage Using Nanotechnology (7)

Smart grids are updated power networks that make use of digital technology to improve electricity distribution in terms of efficiency, reliability, and environmental friendliness. Smart grids are making use of nanotechnology to improve energy storage.

a. State-of-the-Art Grid-Scale Batteries: Grid-scale batteries used in smart grids can have their performance enhanced with the use of nanomaterials. Renewable energy surpluses can be stored in these batteries and released at a later time.

B. Superconductors Made From Nanomaterials: High-temperature superconductors made from nanomaterials are being researched because of their potential to drastically cut down on energy waste during the transmission and distribution of electricity.

c. Sensors for the Smart Grid: Smart grids utilise nanoscale sensors for power monitoring, defect detection, and efficiency enhancement. These sensors supply information in real time, which improves grid administration and servicing.8. Problems and Possible Solutions

Nanotechnology has presented exciting new opportunities for the storage and conversion of energy, but there are also a number of obstacles and potential future approaches to think about. Expandability (a) It is still difficult to mass produce nanomaterials for use in energy applications. Both scalability and efficiency in terms of cost should be prioritised.b. Repercussions on the Environment: It is crucial to fully grasp and ameliorate the environmental impact of nanomaterial manufacturing, usage, and disposal.

# Chapter 6.
# The Role of Nanotechnology in Ecological Repairs

## 6.1- Nanotech applications for pollution control

Nanotechnology's Groundbreaking Role in Pollution Prevention

The environmental and public health risks posed by pollution are significant and increasing. Our earth faces many types of pollution, including air pollution from factories and cars and water pollution from farming and sewage treatment plants. Nanotechnology, however, has emerged as a significant ally in the fight against pollution in the midst of all these environmental challenges. Nanotechnology's ability to manipulate materials at the nanoscale will make it an invaluable tool in the fight against pollution. This essay delves into the intriguing world of nanotech applications for pollution control across several environmental domains, investigating the great potential to address some of the most serious concerns of our time.

1. Preventing Air Pollution

Emissions from transportation, industry, and agriculture are the leading causes of air pollution around the world, which has devastating effects on people's health and the natural environment. Numerous options for reducing air pollution can be found in nanotechnology:

a. Air Filters Made From Nanomaterials Nanotechnology-based air filters can effectively remove numerous airborne contaminants. Nanomaterials, such as carbon nanotubes and metal-organic frameworks, are commonly used in these filters because of their exceptional surface area and adsorption capability. They are efficient at removing airborne contaminants such hazardous particles, VOCs, and metals.

Two words: b. catalytic converters. Catalytic converters play a crucial role in the vehicle industry by lowering emissions. through adding tiny catalysts, typically constituted of platinum nanoparticles, the construction of highly effective catalytic converters has been made possible through nanotechnology. Nitrogen oxides (NOx) and carbon monoxide (CO) can be converted into less dangerous chemicals with the help of these catalysts.

As for c. photocatalysis: Titanium dioxide nanoparticles, for example, are one type of photocatalytic nanomaterial that can be incorporated into the surfaces of buildings and roadways. These materials, when exposed to sunshine, degrade air contaminants into inert chemicals. By reducing the effects of emissions from vehicles and industrial activities, this strategy can considerably lower urban air pollution levels.

Nanosensors, d. It is possible for nanoscale sensors to enable continuous monitoring of air quality. These sensors can detect pollutants at extremely low concentrations, allowing for more efficient pollution management tactics and the introduction of remediation measures at just the right time.

Second, preventing water pollution,

Water pollution is a widespread problem that endangers aquatic ecosystems and human communities. It is caused by a variety of sources, including industrial discharges, agricultural runoff, and insufficient wastewater treatment. Nanotechnology is rapidly becoming an indispensable resource for combating water pollution.

a. Filtration Utilising Nanomaterials: Water purification systems have been greatly improved because to nanomaterials like graphene oxide and carbon nanotubes. Heavy metals, organic pollutants, and bacteria can all be effectively removed from water by using these materials to produce cutting-edge filtration membranes.

b. The Use of Nanoparticles in Water Purification: Iron oxide nanoparticles are just one type of nanoparticle that has shown promise in water purification. Through coagulation, flocculation, and other mechanisms, these particles can absorb organic pollutants and heavy metals in water and make their removal easier.

Catalysts at the Nanoscale c. The advanced oxidation processes (AOPs) utilised to degrade organic contaminants in water rely heavily on nanoscale catalysts. These catalysts produce highly reactive species that are capable of oxidising and destroying pollutants, resulting in potable water that is safer to drink.

Water quality monitoring nanosensors allow for the immediate identification of waterborne pollutants, allowing for more effective cleanup and protection of drinking water supplies.

3. Preventing Soil Pollution

Industrial activities, inappropriate waste disposal, and agricultural practises can all contribute to soil pollution, which in turn can have serious consequences for ecosystems and human health. There are multiple ways in which nanotechnology aids in the fight against soil pollution.

As for a. nanoremediation: Nanoparticles are used in nanoremediation to reduce the impact of contaminated soil. Soil can be made less toxic and less hazardous for both the environment and human populations by using zero-valent iron nanoparticles, for example, to decrease or immobilise heavy metals and organic contaminants.

Stabilising the soil, b. Soil contamination can be contained and exposure to harmful pollutants lessened with the use of nanomaterials. This method prevents contaminants from spreading into groundwater or affecting the surrounding environment.

d. Soil Sensing Devices: Changes in soil properties and the presence of contaminants can be detected using nanoscale sensors developed for in-situ soil quality monitoring. These sensors are crucial because they enable the collection of data in real time, which is essential for the timely implementation of solutions to reduce soil contamination.

(4) Reducing Noise Pollution

Noise pollution has negative consequences on people's health and happiness, and its significance is frequently understated. Ingenious new applications of nanotechnology are being found in the fight against noise pollution.

Soundproofing using Nanomaterials: a. Sound-dampening materials can have their acoustic performance improved by incorporating nanomaterials. Construction, soundproofing, and noise barriers made from these materials offer sophisticated nano-engineered structures that reduce noise propagation and improve acoustic comfort in congested metropolitan areas.

5. Measures to Reduce Light Pollution

Light pollution is a developing problem that has negative consequences on ecosystems, human health, and astronomy; nanotechnology is being used to combat this.

Filters for light made from nanomaterials: a. Nanomaterials are incorporated into light filters and coatings to reduce light pollution. Artificial lighting is less of an intrusion on the environment when certain materials are used because they are designed to selectively block or scatter certain wavelengths of light.The Future of Nanotechnology in Pollution Control and Its Challenges Nanotechnology offers promising new approaches to pollution management, but to fully realise its potential, various obstacles and potential future avenues must be overcome.

a. Toxicology and Risk Assessment Nanomaterials have the potential to significantly improve pollution control efforts, but their effects on the environment and human health must be thoroughly studied. To ensure their appropriate use, it is crucial to better understand and regulate the safety of these materials.

Expandability (b) Nanotech solutions can only be truly beneficial if they can be mass-produced and implemented without breaking the bank. Scalability is essential for these solutions to be widely adopted and used.

c. Destiny in Nature: To lessen unwanted effects, knowing where nanomaterials go and how they get there is crucial. If we don't want nanomaterials to build up in ecosystems and have a harmful impact on the environment, we need to learn more about how they behave.

Collaboration Across Disciplines (d) Scientists, engineers, policymakers, and stakeholders must all work together on pollution prevention. Pollution poses complex and interwoven difficulties, and tackling them will need cooperation across various groups.

e. Regulatory Structures: The use of nanomaterials in pollution management should be governed by strict regulatory frameworks. These structures will guarantee the secure, accountable, and well-regulated use of nanotechnology in pollution management.

f. Raising Consciences: It is crucial to educate the public on the many advantages of nanotech pollution control systems. The public's backing and comprehension are crucial to the effective rollout of these novel methods. Nanotechnology has the potential to play a critical role in solving some of the world's most intractable environmental problems. We may look forward to a cleaner, healthier, and more sustainable future thanks to the fantastic solutions offered by nanotech applications for pollution control as this field continues to evolve.

## 6.2- Water purification and air filtration using nanomaterials

Nanomaterials are reshaping water filtration and air purification.

Clean water and clean air are essential to a healthy and sustainable environment. Pollution and toxins pose a threat to important resources like clean water and air, which are vital to human survival. The manipulation of materials at the nanoscale, known as nanotechnology, has emerged as a potent technique for tackling these issues. This article focuses on the revolutionary effects of nanomaterials in water purification and air filtration, highlighting their applications, benefits, and potential to radically alter our approach to protecting the environment and human health.

Nanomaterials for Water Purification

One of the most basic human rights is the availability of clean water to drink. The poisoning of water supplies, however, is a worldwide issue. When used to water purification issues, nanomaterials have proven to be extremely useful.

1. Filtration membranes made from nanomaterials

Thanks to nanotechnology, cutting-edge filtration membranes have been created that can efficiently filter out a wide variety of water pollutants. Nanomaterials like graphene oxide and carbon nanotubes are commonly used in the fabrication of these membranes. Due to their nanoscale form, these materials have a large surface area, making them effective at entrapping microbes, toxins, and other pollutants.

The advantages of filtration membranes made from nanomaterials include: Nanomaterials' ability to ensnare submicron particles and impurities results in increased filtration efficiency.

The mechanical strength and lifespan of filtration membranes can be improved by using nanomaterials.
- Lower maintenance costs: filters that are more effective last longer and need to be replaced less often.
Fewer filter replacements mean less trash, which is great news for the environment.

Using Nanoparticles to Clean Water

The use of nanoparticles in purifying water is essential. Their many uses include, but are not limited to:

Adsorption (a) High adsorption capacity is a characteristic shared by nanoparticles. Heavy metals and organic pollutants are no match for their ability to bind to and be removed from water.

The Processes of Coagulation and Flocculation: The aggregation of particles and pollutants in water, known as coagulation and flocculation, can be aided by the presence of nanoparticles. This results in larger flocs that can be easily eliminated by settling.

c) Oxidation Titanium dioxide ($TiO_2$) nanoparticles are one type of photocatalytic nanoparticle. Organic water contaminants can be oxidised and broken down by the highly reactive species produced when they are exposed to light.

The antibacterial characteristics of silver nanoparticles and other nanomaterials make them ideal for use in disinfection processes. They can be used to purify water by eliminating harmful microorganisms.

Advanced Oxidation Processes Using Nanoscale Catalysts

The use of AOPs, or advanced oxidation processes, is a cutting-edge technique for purifying water. To degrade organic contaminants, they produce extremely reactive hydroxyl radicals (•OH). Nanoscale catalysts, often made of zero-valent iron, iron oxide, or titanium dioxide, boost AOPs by increasing the rate at which hydroxyl radicals are produced.

Nanoscale catalysts have many benefits when applied to water purification, including:

Nanocatalysts dramatically speed up the rate at which pollutants are broken down, thanks to their increased oxidation efficiency.
Nanocatalysts are flexible and can be applied to the treatment of numerous organic contaminants.
AOPs including nanocatalysts reduce the amount of chemicals needed for treatment.
Fewer hazardous byproducts are produced because pollutants degrade quickly.

4. Nanosensors for Continuously Monitoring Water Quality

Nanosensors have completely altered the way we track water quality. These compact instruments have several uses because of their ability to detect and measure pollutants in water at extremely low concentrations.

Nanosensors' constant data flow enables rapid response to contamination incidents.
Nanosensors have a much higher detection limit, so that even trace amounts of pollution can be identified.
Nanosensors allow for early intervention and rapid response to water quality issues, making them ideal for use in early warning systems.
Saving money on costly water treatment is one benefit of increased monitoring accuracy.

Nanomaterials for Air Filtration

The safety and wellbeing of people and the planet depend on clean air. Negative impacts on respiratory health have been linked to poor air quality, which is often the result of pollutants, allergies, and particle matter. Air filtration systems are benefiting greatly from the incorporation of nanomaterials.

1. Air filters made from nanomaterials

The effectiveness of air filtration devices has been greatly improved thanks to nanomaterials. Carbon nanotubes and metal-organic frameworks are only two examples of the nanomaterials that can be used to create effective air filters. The benefits of using these filters are numerous:

Nanomaterials have a larger surface area and are able to trap tiny particles, leading to enhanced filtration efficiency.
Nanomaterial-based filters are designed to last longer and require less servicing.
Cleaner and healthier indoor air is the result of effective pollution control.
Longer filter lifetimes save energy because there is less need to replace and dispose of filters.

2. Catalytic Converters

Catalytic converters are an essential part of the automotive industry because of their role in lowering emissions. The integration of tiny catalysts, typically consisting of platinum nanoparticles, has allowed for the development of highly effective catalytic converters thanks to nanotechnology. Nitrogen oxides (NOx) and carbon monoxide (CO) can be converted into less dangerous chemicals with the help of these catalysts.

Incorporating nanoparticles into catalytic converters has many advantages.

The efficiency of catalytic converters is increased by the use of nanoscale catalysts, leading to greater NOx and CO reduction. Lower emissions mean cleaner air inside the car, which translates to better gas mileage.
Better air quality and less pollution result from less hazardous emissions, protecting the environment.

Third, the Use of Photocatalysis in Cleaning the Air

Nanomaterials with photocatalytic characteristics, such titanium dioxide nanoparticles, can be used in a process called photocatalysis to degrade air pollutants when exposed to light. This technology can be used for everything from air filtration to making buildings clean themselves. Among photocatalysis' many benefits for cleaning the air are:Photocatalytic nanomaterials degrade pollutants by converting them into inert molecules.
Surfaces covered with photocatalytic nanoparticles can clean themselves, contributing to a more hygienic and less polluted environment.Less regular cleaning and maintenance is needed for self-cleaning surfaces.4. Nanosensors for Monitoring Air Quality

The development of nanosensors specifically for measuring air quality has significantly improved our ability to quantify and regulate pollution levels. These sensors can give real-time data for monitoring purposes and identify a wide variety of airborne pollutants at low concentrations.Some of the advantages of using nanosensors to track air quality are:Nanosensors provide real-time data, allowing for speedy reactions to air quality problems.
Nanosensors can be used as early warning systems for pollution events since they can detect contaminants at extremely low concentrations.Monitoring air quality can help reduce exposure to contaminants, which has positive effects on public health.Directions for the Future and Current ChallengesSeveral problems and future approaches must be explored to fully realise the potential of nanomaterials for use in water purification and air filtration.

# Chapter 7.
# The Role of Nanotechnology in Production

## 7.1- Nanofabrication techniques and 3D printing

Pioneering the Future of Manufacturing with Nanofabrication and 3D Printing

Thanks to developments in nanotechnology and 3D printing, the manufacturing and fabrication industries are undergoing a dramatic revolution. Intricate microdevices and huge macro-scale constructions alike are all benefiting from these new technologies. The ideas, uses, and far-reaching effects of nanofabrication and 3D printing on fields as diverse as aerospace and healthcare will be discussed in this article.

Acquiring Knowledge of Nanofabrication

Nanofabrication is the practise of making things at the nanoscale (usually between one and one hundred nanometers), whether they be structures, materials, or gadgets. At the nanoscale, quantum mechanics rules, and material properties can be very different from their macroscopic analogues. Nanofabrication methods allow for extremely fine-grained control of matter on such a small scale, which has enormous practical implications.

1. Nanofabrication from the Top Down

The first step in top-down nanofabrication is scaling down a large material sample to the nanometer range. In this method, the desired structure is created using subtractive procedures, in which existing material is either removed or altered. Top-down nanofabrication includes the following methods:
As for a. photolithography: In this method, a photoresist (a light-sensitive substance) is exposed through a patterned mask. The

pattern on the mask is transferred to the photoresist using ultraviolet light, leaving a permanent imprint. It's a must-have for making chips and other semiconductors.

electron beam lithography (EBL) With EBL, a concentrated beam of electrons is utilised to etch designs onto a surface. It's great for specific uses and study because of its high resolution and precision.

Microscopy with a Scanning Probe (c) Scanning tunnelling microscopy (STM) and atomic force microscopy (AFM) allow researchers to control and examine materials on the atomic and molecular scales. They are extremely helpful for studying and characterising nanoscale structures.

In a nutshell, nanoimprint lithography d This method involves physically pressing a mould into a substance to create multiple copies of a pattern. It is amenable to mass production because of its simplicity and scalability.

Second-Generation Bottom-Up Nanofabrication

On the other hand, structures are constructed using bottom-up nanofabrication by adding individual atoms or molecules. In many cases, this requires nanoscale materials to self-assemble or be grown in a controlled fashion. Bottom-up nanofabrication includes the following methods:

a. Chemical Vapour Deposition (CVD): Thin films of materials are grown using CVD on a substrate. Atoms are deposited onto the substrate's surface by injecting precursor gases into a chamber and regulating the temperature and pressure. It plays a crucial role in the fabrication of coatings and electronic thin films.

b Molecular Beam Epitaxy (MBE): MBE is a technique for the atomically precise deposition of high-quality thin films of many different materials. It plays an essential role in the fabrication of semiconductors and high-tech materials.

Assembly by Itself (c) Making molecules interact and organise themselves into certain shapes is the goal of self-assembly processes. In DNA nanotechnology, for instance, DNA strands are manipulated to take on certain 3D shapes and configurations on the nanoscale.

d. Synthesis of Nanoparticles: Nanoparticles with tailored characteristics can be synthesised by a variety of techniques, including sol-gel synthesis. Catalysis, drug delivery, and nanocomposites are just a few of the many uses discovered for these tiny particles.

Nanofabrication Use Cases

There are many areas where nanofabrication has proven useful.

Industry of Electronics and Semiconductors, No. 1: The creation of ever-smaller and more powerful electronic components relies heavily on nanofabrication, which is at the heart of the semiconductor industry. It's the driving force behind the development of semiconductors, logic gates, and computer chips.

Second, Healthcare and Medicine: Nanoparticles for drug delivery, microscale medical devices, and biosensors for diagnostics: all made possible by nanofabrication processes.

The Third Energy: Nanofabrication is utilised to develop superior materials for use in energy-related applications such as batteries, fuel cells, and solar cells, all of which contribute to the development of more effective and long-lasting power sources.
Science of Materials, Number Four Nanofabrication's promise has been demonstrated by the creation of novel nanomaterials with novel

properties, such as graphene and carbon nanotubes. Uses for these materials range from aeronautical engineering to consumer electronics.

## Acquiring Knowledge of 3D Printing

Creating three-dimensional objects by adding material layers by layers is known as 3D printing or additive manufacturing. 3D printing creates an object layer by layer, rather than by cutting away excess material as in traditional subtractive manufacturing. The simplicity with which this technology can make sophisticated and individually tailored products has contributed greatly to its rise to prominence.

## Basics of Three-Dimensional Printing

Three-dimensional printing starts with these fundamentals:

1. Layout: Making a 3D digital model of the product is the first stage in the 3D printing process. The 3D printer can follow the instructions for making this model.

The digital model is sliced into thin horizontal layers using specialised software, which are referred to as slices or layers. This is a critical stage since it controls how the printer moves and deposits material for each layer.

Third, in Printing: The 3D printer takes in the sliced design and gradually builds the object from the bottom up. Plastics, metals, ceramics, and even biological materials in the case of bioprinting are all viable options for its utilisation.

4. Post-Production: Cleaning, support removal, and surface finishing are all examples of post-printing processes that could improve an object's quality and use.

# Technologies for creating three-dimensional objects

There are a number of different 3D printing technologies available today, each with its own strengths and weaknesses. The following are some of the most widely used methods of 3D printing:

a. Fused Deposition Modelling (FDM) FDM is widely used in the 3D printing industry. The process includes depositing material layer by layer by extruding thermoplastic filament through a heated nozzle. FDM is popular in both the amateur and commercial sectors.

SLA (Stereolithography) b. In SLA, a vat of liquid photopolymer resin is solidified layer by layer using an ultraviolet (UV) laser. Its great resolution and accuracy make it ideal for constructing things with a lot of fine detail.

c. Selective Laser Sintering (SLS) Layer by layer, powdered materials like polymers, metals, and ceramics are sintered using a laser in SLS. It's an adaptable technology that can be implemented in a number of settings.

d. DLP (Digital Light Processing): In comparison to standard SLA, DLP is considerably quicker because it cures the resin in one continuous layer using a digital light projector.

e for Binder Jetting For 3D printing, binder jetting uses powder. Layers of powder are formed by applying a liquid binding agent on top of the powder. Excess powder is usually removed during post-processing of the printed item.

f. 3D Printing in Metal Direct Metal Laser Sintering (DMLS) and Electron Beam Melting (EBM) are two examples of metal 3D printing methods.

## 7.2- Nanotechnology's role in improving manufacturing processes

Nanotechnology's Impact on Enhanced Production

Manufacturing has entered a new era thanks to nanotechnology, the manipulation of materials at the nanoscale. This cutting-edge innovation is revolutionising manufacturing by allowing for greater precision, efficiency, and personalization in the design, production, and assembly of goods. In this essay, we will examine the significance of nanotechnology in modern manufacturing, including its uses, advantages, and far-reaching effects.

The Heart of Nanotechnology for Industrial Applications

Nanotechnology deals with structures and materials on the nanoscale, which is typically between one to one hundred nanometers in size. Material characteristics can vary greatly from their macroscopic values at this scale. Nanotechnology offers new ways to improve production by altering and modifying materials at the nanoscale. Nanotechnology is having a profound impact on the manufacturing industry primarily in the following ways:

1. Construction and Synthesis of Materials New materials with better qualities including strength, thermal conductivity, and electrical conductivity can be fabricated using nanotechnology. The aerospace and electronics sectors are just two of many that make use of these materials.

Second, Precision Manufacturing is possible because of how well matter can be controlled on the nanoscale, allowing for the creation of delicate and micro-scale components. Producing electronics, medical equipment, and cutting-edge materials with this degree of accuracy is a huge boon.Functional Coatings, Thirdly: Thanks to advancements in nanotechnology, special functional coatings with features like superhydrophobic and superoleophobic characteristics can now be created. Self-cleaning materials and high-tech protective coatings are two areas where these coatings are put to use.

4. Composites Constructed From Nanomaterials Composites' mechanical, electrical, and thermal properties can be improved by using nanomaterials like graphene and carbon nanotubes. Composites like these have numerous applications, including in aviation, automobiles, and building construction.

Nanoelectronics, number 5. Nanotechnology's use in miniaturising electronic components has resulted in more compact and powerful gadgets, from microprocessors to memory storage.

The Use of Nanotechnology in the Creation of New Materials

The ability to design and synthesise new materials is a major aspect in which nanotechnology is enhancing manufacturing processes. Materials can have their properties modified by scientists and engineers at the nanoscale. Nanomaterials are making an impact in many different fields.

High-Tech Composites, 1. Composite materials are increasingly incorporating nanomaterials like carbon nanotubes and graphene due to their superior strength, thermal conductivity, and electrical characteristics. The lightweight and high-performance of these composites make them ideal for usage in aerospace and automotive applications.

Drug Delivery Using Nanoparticles: Drugs are delivered with greater efficiency and specificity using nanoparticles in the pharmaceutical business. Functionalizing nanoparticles allows for targeted drug delivery, which improves treatment outcomes.Better battery technology and other forms of energy storage Advanced battery materials, such as nanoscale lithium-ion batteries, have been developed thanks to developments in nanotechnology. There is a greater energy density, a longer cycle life, and quicker charging times with these materials.

Enhanced Catalysis, Number Four Nanomaterials are utilised as catalysts because they improve the efficiency and selectivity of chemical reactions. To make fuels, chemicals, and other industrial goods, these catalysts are indispensable.

Nanocomposites, number five: Nanocomposites with improved mechanical and electrical properties are being developed by incorporating nanomaterials into polymers and other materials. The automotive, aerospace, and construction industries are just a few that put these materials to good use.

Nanotechnology and ultra-precise mechanical assembly

Manipulating matter at the atomic and molecular levels, as is possible with nanotechnology, allows for extremely precise production. This degree of regulation is particularly important in the following fields:

Electronics, No. 1 Nanoscale accuracy is extremely useful in the electronics sector. As electronic components continue to shrink in size, we are able to build more powerful and compact integrated circuits and microprocessors.

Microfabrication, secondly: Microelectromechanical systems (MEMS) and other microdevices are made using microfabrication techniques for a wide range of uses. Sensors, actuators, and even medical equipment rely on these devices.

Modern Production Methods, Third Electron beam lithography and focused ion beam (FIB) machining are only two examples of the state-of-the-art manufacturing methods made possible by nanotechnology. Industries including aerospace and healthcare use these methods to make precision components.

4. Biomedical Equipment: Engineering on a nanoscale scale is essential for the creation of high-precision medical equipment including drug delivery systems and diagnostic instruments. These applications rely heavily on nanoparticles and nanosensors.

Nanotechnology has helped advance additive manufacturing techniques like 3D printing. 3D printers can build items with greater resolution and precision when nanoscale materials are used. Numerous sectors, from aircraft to healthcare, make use of this technology.

Coatings that serve a purpose and surface engineering

Functional coatings and surface engineering have entered uncharted territory thanks to advancements in nanotechnology. Superhydrophobicity and superoleophobicity are two extraordinary qualities that can be achieved by altering the surfaces of materials on the nanoscale. The following are some of the fields that benefit from these coatings:

To begin with, Self-Cleaning Surfaces Surfaces coated with superhydrophobic materials are virtually self-cleaning because water and the particles and pollutants it carries are repelled. The coatings are applied on glass, fabrics, and construction materials.

Anti-fouling coatings, secondly: Ship hulls protected by superoleophobic coatings are less likely to become encrusted with barnacles and other marine creatures. In doing so, you save on both drag and gas.

Thirdly, Anti-Corrosion Coatings: Metals with anti-corrosion coatings made with nanotechnology. Coatings like these prevent corrosion and increase the useful life of infrastructure like bridges, pipelines, and aeroplanes.Optical Coatings, Number Four: Optical coatings made with nanotechnology decrease reflection, glare, and light loss in lenses, mirrors, and screens.

Bioactive coatings, number five: Nanotechnology has been used to coat medical implants and equipment with bioactive materials that stimulate tissue growth.Nanotechnology's Potential Industrial Uses

The effects of nanotechnology on production are far-reaching, having applications in many fields.Aerospace: 1. Advanced materials, such as carbon nanotube-reinforced composites, help the aerospace industry cut aircraft weight and improve fuel efficiency.

Motor vehicles: Nanotechnology has aided the automotive industry in creating lighter materials, more efficient engines, and safer vehicles.

Nanotechnology has allowed for the miniaturisation of electrical components, which has resulted in smaller and more powerful devices in the electronics industry.

The Healthcare System Medical gadgets, drug delivery systems, and diagnostic equipment that utilise nanotechnology and precision manufacturing have been shown to enhance patient care.

5. Energy: Nanotechnology is instrumental in the creation of cutting-edge materials for batteries, solar cells, and fuel cells, all of which contribute to more environmentally friendly forms of energy production.Sixth, Building: Self-cleaning and anti-corrosion coatings for building materials are made possible by nanotechnology, which is employed in construction to save money on upkeep.

Fabrics, number seven: Fabrics treated with nanotechnology may now repel water and resist stains, greatly improving their practicality.

# Chapter 8.
# Concerns Over the Use of Nanotechnology

## 8.1- Ethical considerations in nanotech research

Moral Concerns Regarding Nanotechnology Study

Several industries, from medicine to electronics, have benefited greatly from nanotechnology's ability to manipulate and engineer materials at the nanoscale. Research in the field of nanotechnology has enormous potential, but with that ability comes enormous responsibility. Ethical issues are more important as nanotechnology develops to ensure that its benefits are used properly and its risks are kept to a minimum. Ethical issues and values that guide scientists, policymakers, and society as a whole will be examined as we delve into the ethical considerations in nanotechnology research.

Nanotechnology: Possibilities and Threats

It's possible that nanotechnology will completely transform our society. From fighting disease to improving the environment, it provides answers to some of the world's most serious problems. Nanotechnology research holds many potential benefits:

Healthcare Improvements 1. Drugs may now be administered with pinpoint accuracy, diseases can be diagnosed at an earlier stage, and damaged tissue can be repaired using nanotechnology.

Second, Environmental Sustainability Is being worked on by creating nanotech applications for cleaner water, less pollution, and more effective solar panels.

Third, Modern Electronics: Nanotechnology allows for the development of smaller and more powerful electrical devices such as computers and sensors.

4. Energy Efficiency: Nanomaterials help with better energy storage and conversion, which lowers energy usage and has a positive effect on the environment.

These benefits, however, are not without the risk of harm or ethical difficulties:

First, Ecological Issues: Concerns have been raised concerning the potential long-term effects and harm to ecosystems from the release of nanoparticles into the environment.

Safety and Health Second: Nanoparticle exposure and its consequences on human health are still poorly understood. There is a serious moral problem with not making sure nanomaterials and goods are safe.

Threats to Security, Part 3 Nanotechnology's potential for both good and evil uses raises moral questions. It has both legitimate and malicious applications, and is therefore potentially dangerous.

Fourth, Equity and Access: It is morally important to ensure that the benefits of nanotechnology are distributed fairly so as not to worsen existing socioeconomic disparities.

Important Ethical Questions Regarding Nanotechnology Research

Nanotechnology research relies heavily on a number of moral factors, including:

Accountability and Openness to the Public (1): Researchers and academic institutions working in the field of nanotechnology have a responsibility to be forthright about the benefits and hazards of their projects. Holding researchers and developers accountable guarantees ethical behaviour in the field.

Second, researchers should be mindful of the ecological effects of nanotechnology. The creation of environmentally friendly nanomaterials and other environmentally sustainable practises is crucial.

Third, the well-being of people: Employee, customer, and citizen safety must always come first. Any potential health risks must be thoroughly evaluated and preventative measures put in place.

4. Consent After Full Disclosure: Getting people's informed consent is essential in the medical and research fields. People should be provided full disclosure and informed consent on the medical and scientific applications of nanotechnology.

5. Confidentiality: Nanotechnology data collection might compromise personal information. In the era of nanosensors and data collection, it is imperative that moral norms be created to safeguard the privacy of individuals.

6. The Conundrum of Dual Use: Because the same technology can be used for both good and evil, researchers, politicians, and society as a whole have a responsibility to confront the potential dangers of nanotechnology. Misuse can be reduced with the use of rules and regulations.

The benefits of nanotechnology should be shared fairly between all people and all cultures. This brings us to our seventh and last point:
7. Equity and Access:. Nanotechnology advancements shouldn't be off-limits to the general public.

8. Ethical Regulation: Research and development should be subjected to independent ethical supervision organisations and review systems. These groups can make sure that ethical norms are followed and that any problems with ethics are dealt with.
Some Ethical Difficulties Associated with Nanotechnology Research

Here are a few instances to help illustrate the ethical dilemmas that arise with nanotechnology research:

1. The Risks of Nanomaterials The potential dangers of nanoparticles are a major ethical conundrum in the field of nanotechnology. Even while nanoparticles' special qualities make them useful in many contexts, there is grounds for concern about their potential toxicity. In order to safely handle and dispose of nanomaterials, researchers need to thoroughly evaluate the potential dangers involved.

Second, the effect on the environment: The effects of releasing nanomaterials into the environment may not be immediately apparent. Threats to ecosystems, animals, and people's health are all things to think about while evaluating ethics. To reduce these dangers, environmental monitoring and responsible waste disposal are essential.

Safety and Confidentiality: Privacy issues have been brought up in relation to nanotechnology, especially nanosensors and surveillance systems. Nanoscale data collection and analysis has the potential to invade personal space. To find a happy medium between technology progress and individual privacy, rules of conduct are required.

(4) Medical Applications of Informed Consent Nanotechnology has several applications in healthcare and medical research, including in diagnosis, drug delivery, and treatment. When patients participate in studies or therapies involving nanotechnology, informed consent is crucial. The patient must voluntarily agree to the procedure after being informed of all of the possible outcomes.

5. The Problem with Dual Use and Security: Nanotechnology raises moral questions due to its potential for dual use. Both benign and malicious applications of nanotechnology are possible. To prevent the abuse of nanotech developments, researchers and governments must traverse these challenges.

# Approaches to Handling Moral Questions Raised by Nanotechnology Study

Research with nanotechnology necessitates a diverse strategy to address ethical concerns:

(1) Working with people from other disciplines: It is important to include scholars, ethicists, policymakers, business leaders, and the general public in ethical conversations. The identification of ethical concerns and the creation of plans to solve them can benefit from a multidisciplinary perspective.

Ethical Principles and Standards Creating nanotechnology-specific ethical norms is crucial. Principles and criteria for ethical research and development should be laid forth clearly in these guidelines.

Thirdly, Ethical Supervision: Research initiatives can have their ethical consequences evaluated by impartial ethics committees or review boards. These regulatory agencies are helpful because they may offer advice and help keep ethics high.

(4) Involving the Public: Discussing the moral implications of nanotechnology with the general public is essential. Ethical rules are more likely to reflect social norms if they are developed with public involvement.

5.Governance and Regulation: The usage of nanotechnology necessitates the creation of regulatory frameworks by policymakers. Safety, environmental, and ethical research norms can all be established by legislation.

Researchers and practitioners in the nanotech field should be educated and trained on ethical problems and responsible behaviour (6. Education and Training). Responsible research requires a grasp of and familiarity with ethical considerations.

7. Ethical Impact Assessment: It is important to consider the potential ethical implications of nanotechnology research programmes and applications. These evaluations can help with making moral choices and ensuring that nanotechnology advances in a responsible manner.

Conclusion

There is no denying nanotechnology's potential to revolutionise many industries for the better. Ethical concerns are also important in nanotechnology research. Safety, environmental effect, privacy problems, and dual-use dilemmas are all examples of ethical challenges that need thoughtful and accountable responses. Researchers, governments, and the general public must work together to ensure that nanotechnology research is conducted in accordance with ethical standards that advance societal priorities including human and environmental health. Leveraging the full potential of requires careful development and ethical oversight.

## 8.2- Safety precautions and regulations in nanotechnology

Regulations and Precautions for Nanotechnology Safety

Nanotechnology, the manipulation of matter at the nanoscale, has revolutionised a wide range of sectors by providing novel approaches to addressing some of the world's most intractable problems. Researchers, employees, and the environment all have reason to be wary of nanoparticles because of their unusual features. Strong safety precautions and regulations are necessary for the ethical advancement and implementation of nanotechnology. This article will delve into the topic of nanotechnology safety and regulations, discussing the hazards, countermeasures, and oversight organisations involved in this revolutionary sector.

Nanotechnology: Its Potential Benefits and Threats

The medical, electronic, energy, and materials sciences are just a few of the fields that have benefited greatly from the applications made possible by nanotechnology. It can be used for anything from solar panels that are very efficient to lightweight and durable materials that can be used for targeted medicine delivery. There is a wide range of potential advantages:

First, in the field of medicine, nanotechnology is paving the way for game-changing advances in drug delivery systems, diagnostics, and regenerative medicine.

Environmental Solutions 2: Nanotechnology offers new ways to tackle environmental problems, such as advanced water and air purification systems and alternative energy sources.

Electonics, third: Nanotechnology allows for the development of smaller and more powerful electrical components such as microprocessors and memory storage.

Science of Materials (4) Graphene and carbon nanotubes are only two examples of nanomaterials that are boosting innovation in a wide range of fields by improving the mechanical, electrical, and thermal capabilities of other materials.

However, new dangers arise due to the nanoscale specificity of nanomaterials' features and behaviour:

Safety and Health Issues Concerns about the safety of nanomaterials for researchers, employees, and end-users have been raised because to the possibility that they may exhibit unforeseen biological and toxicological effects.

Impact on the Environment: Unknown effects on ecosystems and human health may result from the release of nanoparticles into the environment.

Ethical Conundrums 3. Since the same nanotechnology that has peaceful benefits may also be exploited for military or malicious goals, its dual-use nature offers ethical issues.

The rapid development of nanotechnology has led to regulatory gaps that may leave employees, customers, and the environment vulnerable.

Careful Measures for the Future of Nanotechnology

Several safeguards are used to reduce the dangers of developing and researching nanotechnology:

First, Technical Regulations:

Fume extractors and hand protection stations Researchers use protective gear like fume hoods and glove boxes to keep nanoparticles contained.

- Regional Ventilation Systems These devices filter out nanoparticles in the air and release them outside of the building.

Second, use appropriate personal protective equipment (PPE):

To avoid getting nanomaterials on their skin, scientists wear protective gear such lab coats, gloves, and coveralls.

A word about respirators Respiratory protection may be required when working with potentially dangerous nanoparticles to prevent inhalation.

3. Proper Storage and Handling

Protocols for Handling Safe practises for working with, transporting, and storing nanoparticles are codified in detail.

- Safekeeping: Nanomaterials are kept in a clean, dry, and secure environment, in their own, clearly labelled containers.

(4) Analysing Dangers:

Evaluation of Potential Dangers Nanomaterials' potential dangers and toxicity are investigated by a thorough hazard study.

Researchers evaluate the chance of exposure during various tasks and the various routes of exposure, such as inhalation, ingestion, and skin contact.

5. Education and Training:

Researchers and employees in the nanotechnology industry receive specialised safety training to familiarise them with the novel dangers they face and the precautions they must take.

Workers receive education on how to respond in an emergency situation, covering topics like first aid and spill management.

6. Waste Control:

The safe disposal of nanomaterial waste is outlined so that the environment is not harmed in any way.

Reusing and Recycling: Waste and environmental damage can be reduced if measures are taken to recycle and reuse nanoparticles.

7 Ongoing Inspections and Tests:

Inspections of the Workplace: Audits and inspections of the workplace are performed frequently to check for adherence to safety policies and laws.

- Monitoring of Air and Water Quality: Nanoparticle emission and pollution in the workplace can be detected by monitoring air and water quality.

Nanotechnology Regulations

Strong restrictions are needed to address safety concerns and preserve the environment and human health in the fast developing field of nanotechnology. While some jurisdictions have passed laws tailored specifically to nanotech, others have simply included nanomaterials in their current set of rules. Important facets of the law include:

1. Methods for Evaluating and Controlling Dangers

- Risk Assessment and Toxicology Toxicological studies are typically required by regulatory agencies to ascertain the dangers posed by nanoparticles. Potential risks to people and the environment must be considered.

Strategies for Managing Risk: Risk management measures, such as exposure controls and workplace safety practises, may be required by law as a means of reducing the likelihood of harm.

Secondly, reporting and labelling:

Labelling and reporting of products containing nanoparticles may be required by law. - Nanomaterial Identification. Consumers and employees alike benefit from the resulting openness.

Product Safety Information Sheets: Products incorporating nanomaterials may require safety data sheets from their manufacturers outlining their characteristics and correct storage procedures.

Third, a study of the effects on the environment

Environmental Impact Research: Environmental impact assessments may be required by regulatory organisations in order to evaluate risks and apply safeguards for nanomaterials that may have an effect on the environment.

4.Guarantees for Shoppers:

- Consumer Product Safety: There may be rules in place to make sure that items sold to the general public that include nanomaterials are safe to use as intended.

5. Health and Safety in the Workplace

- Standards for Employee Safety Industries that work with nanoparticles may be required to adhere to additional safety regulations. Personal protective equipment (PPE), exposure limits, and safe work procedures are all covered by these regulations.

## 6. Patents and Other Forms of Intellectual Property:

Nanotechnology Product Approval by Government Agencies A nanotech product's patentability and marketability can hinge on whether or not it receives the necessary regulatory permission.

The Function of Governing Agencies

To guarantee that nanotechnology research and applications are safe and environmentally friendly, regulatory organisations play a critical role. Among them are:

Environmental Protection Agencies (EPA): EPA agencies are responsible for controlling the discharge of nanomaterials into the environment and for conducting environmental impact assessments.

Secondly, the Occupational Safety and Health Administrations (OSHA) set norms and requirements to protect workers in settings where nanomaterials are used.

Third, the FDA (Food and Drug Administration): The Food and Drug Administration (FDA) oversees the use of nanotechnology in the healthcare and food industries to ensure patient and consumer safety.

The Commission on the Safety of Consumer Products (CPSC): The CPSC monitors the safety of products on the market that incorporate nanomaterials.

Patent Offices, Number Five: It's possible that patent offices will wait for nanotechnology items to receive regulatory approval before issuing patents.

# Directions for the Future and Current Challenges

However, there are still a number of obstacles to overcome in the realm of nanotechnology safety standards.

The Fast Pace of Technological Developments 1. The establishment of thorough regulations often lags behind the quick speed of technology improvements, leaving regulatory loopholes.

Observation and Regulation

# Chapter 9.
# Nanotechnology Developments and Prospects

## 9.1- Recent breakthroughs and emerging trends

Technological Advances and Future Directions

Technology in today's lightning-fast world is advancing at a rate never before seen. New technological developments and trends are influencing how we live, work, and communicate. The healthcare, transportation, artificial intelligence, and communication industries are just a few that stand to benefit from these developments. To better understand the future we may inhabit, we will examine some of the most significant technological advances and new trends.

First, there's quantum computing.

We are on the threshold of a quantum computer revolution. Quantum computers use quantum bits, also known as qubits, which are capable of being in a number of different states at once to represent information instead of the binary 0s and 1s used by classical computers. As a result, quantum computers may complete difficult tasks at an unprecedented rate when compared to classical computers.

The development of more reliable and error-resistant qubits in recent years has increased the practicality of quantum computers. IBM, Google, and even up-and-coming companies like Rigetti are all developing quantum hardware and software solutions. Despite its infancy, quantum computing already has the potential to revolutionise established industries like cryptography, optimisation, and drug discovery.

2.Machine learning and artificial intelligence

Advances in artificial intelligence (AI) and machine learning are being made in a variety of fields. Recent advances include:

New Generation Natural Language Processing (GPT-3): The GPT-3 language model developed by OpenAI uses deep learning to generate natural-sounding text and comprehend its meaning. This development has ramifications for automated content creation, conversational interfaces, and language translation.

Vision, Computer-Based: Technology like self-driving cars, facial recognition systems, and real-time object detection has been made possible by recent advancements in computer vision. Businesses at the vanguard of this movement include Tesla, Waymo, and NVIDIA.

In games like Go and Dota 2, reinforcement learning algorithms have outperformed human players, demonstrating the potential of AI to tackle challenging real-world issues.

The Role of AI in Medical Care Diagnostics, drug discovery, and medical image analysis are all receiving enhancements thanks to artificial intelligence. Medical practitioners can benefit from using AI models for disease diagnosis and prognosis.

Third, the 5G Technology

The introduction of 5G technology is altering the way we talk to one another. 5G's enhanced data transmission speeds and reduced latency pave the way for new developments in many fields:

AR/VR (Augmented Reality/Virtual Reality) More immersive and responsive AR/VR experiences are only possible with 5G technology.

When it comes to the Internet of Things (5G's high-speed, low-latency connections improve the functionality of IoT devices). This paves the way for driverless vehicles, smart cities, and other industrial Internet of Things uses.

A Look at Telemedicine High-quality telemedicine services, such as remote consultations, surgeries, and patient monitoring, are made possible by 5G in the healthcare industry.

Better Performance on Mobile Devices Download speeds, video playback, and mobile gaming experiences are all enhanced for users.

(4) Biological Engineering and Genetic Modification

Major advances in medicine and farming have resulted from the combination of biotechnology and genetic engineering.

- Gene Editing Using CRISPR-Cas9 The development of CRISPR has lowered the barriers to entry for precise gene editing. It could be used to create GMOs with desirable characteristics or to treat genetic disorders.

Medicine Tailored to the Individual: The results of genetic testing and analysis can be used to create individualised care plans. Treatments for cancer, uncommon diseases, and pharmacogenomics are all benefiting from this new method.

- mRNA Technology and Vaccines The success of mRNA technology in the quick generation of vaccines against COVID-19 shows its promise in combating other infectious diseases.

Automation & Robotics, No. 5

The use of robotics and other forms of automation is expanding across many sectors as these technologies advance.

- Driverless Cars Vehicles capable of driving themselves are getting closer to being available to the public. Businesses at the vanguard of this movement include Tesla, Waymo, and GM.

Automation in Agriculture The use of robots and drones in agriculture has increased productivity and decreased expenses by automating previously labor-intensive processes including planting, harvesting, and crop monitoring.

Robots for Delivery and Inventory Management: Companies like Amazon are utilising autonomous robots for order fulfilment and last-mile delivery, completely altering the landscape of logistics and e-commerce.

Robotics in Healthcare Healthcare facilities are increasingly utilising robots to aid in surgical procedures, patient care, and drug administration.

6. Renewable sources of power and environmentally friendly gadgets

Innovations in renewable energy and environmentally friendly technology have been spurred by the need to combat climate change.

Improvements in solar panel efficiency and declining production costs are making solar energy a viable alternative to conventional power sources.

The Storage of Energy: Lithium-ion batteries, as well as other technologies like solid-state batteries, are essential for the widespread use of renewable energy and the development of electric cars.
In the case of hydrogen fuel cells, Fuel cell vehicles and energy storage are just two of the growing number of uses for hydrogen as a clean energy transporter.

Carbon capture and utilisation (CC&U) technologies are being developed to reduce greenhouse gas emissions from industrial operations by capturing and reusing carbon emissions.

## 7. Interplanetary Travel

There has been a recent boom in space exploration, marked by daring missions and scientific advances.

Private Spaceflight Operators: SpaceX, Blue Origin, and Virgin Galactic are just a few of the companies that are making strides in the commercialization of space travel and settlement.

Recent Mars missions have included NASA's Perseverance rover and the United Arab Emirates' Hope orbiter, both of which are looking at the possibility of human settlement on Mars.

New space telescopes, such as the James Webb Space Telescope, will allow us to see more of the universe and learn more about faraway planets and galaxies.

## The Eighth Most Important Thing to Do for Online Safety

Cybersecurity tools and procedures are advancing at the same rapid rate as the sophistication of cyberattacks.

Zero Trust Security With a zero-trust approach, you can't trust anyone, inside or outside of the company. This method strengthens defences against both internal and external attacks.

AI-Based Safety Measures Cyber threats are identified and countered in real time with the help of machine learning and AI.

Safe Quantum Cryptography. There will be an increasing demand for quantum-safe cryptography as quantum computing develops. In preparation for the post-quantum era, quantum-safe algorithms are being created for data security.

Blockchain technology and distributed financial systems (DeFi) 9.

The use cases for blockchain technologies and cryptocurrencies are expanding:

- Defi-Enabled Platforms: Decentralised finance platforms eliminate the need for middlemen by facilitating financial transactions like lending, borrowing, and selling.

A note on Non-Fungible Tokens In recent years, NFTs have gained popularity as a form of digital representation of value for things like artwork, collectibles, and digital material.

Currency issued by a central bank electronically Digital versions of national currencies are being considered for creation by governments and central banks to promote digital payments and financial inclusion.

10. At the Edge

By moving computation and data storage closer to the point of data creation, edge computing can drastically cut down on latency and make real-time computations possible. It could be used in a number of contexts, including:

Internet of Things and Smart Cities: For real-time processing of data from IoT devices, such as that generated by smart traffic management and energy efficiency applications, edge computing is important.The use of edge computing in autonomous vehicles improves both their safety and their ability to react quickly to changing road conditions.- Delivery of Content:

## 9.2- Predictions for the future of nanotechnology

Nanotechnology's Prognosis for the Future

Medical and technological areas alike have benefited greatly from nanotechnology's ability to manipulate matter at the atomic and molecular scale. We can look forward to incredible advancements that will define the future as this revolutionary technology continues to advance. This article will discuss the possible developments, applications, and consequences of nanotechnology in the future of science, industry, and society.

1. The Emergence of Nanomedicine

The sector of medicine is one that nanotechnology will continue to transform. We can anticipate the following as our knowledge of nanoparticles and their effects on living systems grows:

Targeted Drug Administration: Drugs will have fewer adverse effects and work better with the help of advanced nanoparticles created to target specific cells or regions.

Better results and more effective treatment for diseases including cancer, diabetes, and Alzheimer's will be possible thanks to nanoscale biosensors and imaging techniques.

The Promise of Regenerative Medicine Regenerative medicine and the development of new organs through the use of nanoscale scaffolds and materials may one day render organ transplants obsolete.

Sustainability and Environmental Cleanup

Sustainability and the remediation of environmental problems will be greatly aided by nanotechnology. Future possibilities could include:

To guarantee that people all across the world have access to safe drinking water, scientists are developing filters and membranes made from nanomaterials.

- Air Filtration: Advances in nanotechnology will allow for more effective air filtration systems, resulting in cleaner indoor air and less disease transmission from airborne pollutants and pathogens.

Renewable Resources: The adoption of renewable energy sources will be hastened thanks to the improvements in solar cell and battery efficiency and storage provided by nanomaterials.

New Developments in Computing and Electronics

Advances in nanotechnology will fuel developments across the electronics and computing industries, such as

A Note on Quantum Computing Data processing, cryptography, and intricate simulations will all be radically altered when quantum computing develops and begins to take advantage of qubits' peculiar features.

Please note: Nanoscale Transistors Electronic devices will become even more potent and energy-efficient when nanoelectronics and tiny transistors are developed.

Electronics with a Modular Design Flexible and wearable electronic devices useful in healthcare, communications, and personal computing will be made possible by the incorporation of nanomaterials.

Better Understanding of Materials (#4)

The advent of nanotechnology will aid in the creation of high-tech materials with never-before-seen qualities such as:

Supermaterials, if you will. Advantages in aerospace, construction, and manufacturing could be realised with nanoscale materials tailored for enhanced strength, flexibility, and conductivity.

Materials That Can Heal Themselves: Self-repairing nanomaterials will extend the useful life of items and infrastructure, cutting down on the resources spent on upkeep.

Intelligent Materials: Materials will be equipped with nanoscale sensors and actuators, allowing them to react to their surroundings and evolve over time.

5. Enhanced Energy Generation and Storage

Energy storage and generation technologies will advance thanks to nanotechnology.

Batteries with a High Capacity The use of modern nanomaterials in battery technology will result in dramatic improvements in energy density, charging speed, and battery life.

Energy Sources: Clean and efficient energy conversion, especially in vehicles and fixed power plants, will be made possible by nanotechnology.

Thermoelectric Materials: Nanoscale Engineering will provide extremely efficient thermoelectric materials for converting waste heat into energy, with applications in industries and vehicles.

6. Developments in the Food and Agriculture Sector

The use of nanotechnology will be crucial in solving the world's food and farming problems:
Accurate Farming Practises: In order to optimise agricultural practises and reduce resource consumption, nanoscale sensors and

gadgets will offer real-time data on soil health, crop status, and pest infestations.

Food Preservation and Safety Improved food safety testing can be accomplished in addition to longer food shelf life thanks to the use of nanomaterials in food packaging.

Nutritional Supplements: With the use of nanoscale carriers, farmers will be able to increase crop production and livestock health.

7. Cutting-Edge Production Methods, Like 3D Printing

Nanotechnology will have a profound impact on manufacturing processes, especially in the following areas:

Methods of Nanofabrication: Nanofabrication techniques that are both precise and efficient will allow for the production of complex and individually tailored goods in a variety of sectors.

Nanoscale materials used to 3D printers will allow for the creation of high-resolution, functional things such as medical implants and aeronautical components.

Smart Sensors and the Internet of Things

Nanoscale sensors and gadgets will help advance IoT by allowing for advancements in areas such as

Reduced-Size Sensing Devices: Small, highly sensitive sensors will monitor the surrounding environment, building integrity, and health metrics in real time.

- Energy-Efficient IoT Devices: Electronics based on nanomaterials will increase the responsiveness and battery life of IoT devices.

In a Smart City: Infrastructure, transport, and public services can all benefit from smart city efforts that employ nanotechnology.

Nanosatellites and Space Exploration 9.

The development of nanosatellites and novel propulsion technologies made possible by nanotechnology will propel human space exploration forward.

Miniaturised and efficient components for CubeSats and other tiny satellite platforms will lower the cost and increase the accessibility of space travel thanks to nanosatellites.

Nanotechnology will pave the way for the creation of cutting-edge propulsion technologies, which will make space travel quicker and more efficient.

10 The Moral and Legal Obstacles

There will be moral and legal questions to answer as nanotechnology develops further. Focusing on responsible production and use is essential for resolving concerns about safety, privacy, and security.

11. Problems with Ethics and Government Regulation

There will be moral and legal questions to answer as nanotechnology develops further. Focusing on responsible production and use is essential for resolving concerns about safety, privacy, and security.

Ethical considerations stress the importance of maintaining high standards in nanotechnology study, development, and use. Concerns about privacy, monitoring, and the fair distribution of nanotechnology innovations will all factor into ethical deliberations.

Impact on the Environment: There has to be careful monitoring of nanomaterials' long-term effects as they are released into the environment, and measures will be created to lessen any possible damage to ecosystems.

Health and Safety Notes Potential health concerns connected with exposure to nanomaterials must be protected against for the sake of researchers, workers, and the general public. It will be necessary to create and strictly adhere to safety regulations and safeguards.

Security Concerns The fact that nanotechnology has the potential for both good and evil uses presents difficulties. To reduce abuse, there needs to be regulation and supervision.

- Legal Procedures To keep up with the ever-changing nature of nanotechnology, policymakers will need to create flexible regulatory frameworks that cover concerns like safety, environmental effect, and morality.

Conclusion

Nanotechnology's future is ripe with opportunity and promise. Nanotechnology will continue to revolutionise many fields, from medical and environmental cleanup to electronics and materials research. To make sure nanotechnology lives up to its potential for good for people and the earth, it will face ethical and regulatory issues, which must be tackled with responsible, forward-thinking initiatives. As we approach the beginning of a new era,

# Chapter 10.
# Nanotechnology's Repercussions on Society

## 10.1- How nanotechnology is changing our daily lives

Nanotechnology and Its Effects on Our Everyday Lives

Products we use to the technologies that power our modern world have all been profoundly changed by nanotechnology, the science and engineering of altering matter at the nanoscale. As research into nanotechnology progresses, it will likely improve consumer goods and provide novel approaches to old problems. This article will discuss the ways in which nanotechnology is influencing the present and the future.

1. Electronics Using Nanotechnology

The electronic industry is one of the most obvious beneficiaries of nanotechnology. Miniaturisation of components and the discovery of nanoscale materials have radically altered the form, function, and efficiency of electronic gadgets. Some of the most important ways in which nanotechnology has altered our daily interactions with electronics are as follows:

- Miniaturised and Highly Effective Devices: Devices from smartphones and laptops to wearables have benefited from the miniaturisation made possible by nanotechnology in areas such as transistors and memory storage.

Display Enhancements Quantum dots and other nanoscale materials have played a crucial role in the development of high-resolution, low-power displays for electronics like televisions, tablets, and computer monitors.- Extended Battery Life: Thanks to developments in nanomaterials, the batteries in our mobile devices now last longer, keeping us in touch all day long.

## Nanotechnology in Health Care

Patient care, diagnostics, and medicine delivery are just a few areas where nanotechnology is making significant strides. Among the many modifications are:

Targeted Drug Administration: Drugs can have fewer adverse effects and more favourable outcomes when delivered to the target cells or tissues via nanoparticles. Cancer treatment is just one of several medical uses for this innovation.

The use of nanoscale sensors and imaging techniques has made it possible to diagnose diseases, such as cancer, at an early stage when treatment is likely to have the most impact.

Precise Medical Care: More effective medications with fewer side effects are on the horizon because to nanotechnology's push towards personalised medicine based on a patient's genetic profile.

3. Restoration of Ecological Balance

When it comes to solving environmental problems and fostering a culture of sustainability, nanotechnology is at the forefront.

- Cleaning the Water: Clean drinking water can be provided to areas plagued by pollution and water scarcity by using filters and membranes made from nanomaterials.

Filtration of Air: Improved indoor air quality and public health are the results of the application of cutting-edge nanotechnology in air filtration systems.

Renewable Resources: Renewable energy sources, such as solar panels and batteries, are becoming more efficient and more widely available thanks to advancements in nanotechnology.

Science of Materials, Number Four

New, high-performance materials with unique nanoscale structures are being developed thanks to advancements in nanotechnology. Here are a few of the main shifts:

Supermaterials, if you will. Aerospace, automotive, and construction industries have benefited greatly from the usage of engineered nanomaterials due to their superior strength, flexibility, and conductivity.

Materials That Can Heal Themselves: The development of self-repairing materials made possible by nanotechnology has increased product durability and decreased the need for costly repairs.

Intelligent Materials: By embedding nanoscale sensors and actuators into materials, we can make them more useful and resilient to environmental shifts.

5. Agriculture and Food

Nanotechnology is having a positive effect on the agricultural and food industries, encouraging more sustainable methods of production. Important alterations include:

Accurate Farming Practises: Real-time information on soil conditions, crop health, and pest infestations is made possible by nanoscale sensors and devices, allowing farmers to refine their methods and save money.

Food Preservation and Safety Improved shelf life, lessening of spoilage, and easier testing for food safety are all possible thanks to the usage of nanomaterials in food packaging.

Increased crop yields and better animal health can both result from better nutrient delivery in plants and livestock, which is made possible by nanotechnology.

## 6. Data Transmission and Storage

Communication, information retrieval, and data storage have all been revolutionised thanks to nanotechnology.

Better and quicker communication: Faster internet and more effective worldwide communication have been made possible by the incorporation of nanoscale components into telecoms equipment.

Information Archiving: Thanks to developments in nanotechnology, we now have the ability to store large amounts of data in much smaller and more portable devices.

Smart gadgets and wearable technology: Smart gadgets and wearables benefit from nanomaterial integration because of the increased functionality that results.

## 7 Enhanced Energy Technology

Improvements in energy-related technologies have been greatly aided by nanotechnology.

Batteries with a High Capacity Thanks to advancements in nanotechnology, batteries for EVs and portable electronics are now more powerful and last longer.

Green Power Generation Nanotechnology is improving the efficiency and decreasing the price of renewable energy sources like solar panels and wind turbines, hastening the shift to cleaner, more sustainable energy.

Nanotechnology has made it possible to create more efficient lighting options, such as light-emitting diode (LED) bulbs, which use less electricity and last longer than traditional incandescent bulbs.

## 8. Measurement of Air and Water Quality

Water and air quality monitors that are both highly sensitive and compact have been made possible by advances in nanotechnology.

Sensors for Measuring Water Quality: Contaminants and pathogens in water sources can be detected by nanoscale sensors, making it safe for human consumption.

Sensors for Measuring Air Quality: Integrating nanoscale sensors into IoT devices paves the way for continuous indoor air quality monitoring in homes, offices, and cities.

## 9. Cosmetics and Personal Hygiene

The cosmetics and personal care industries have been greatly impacted by nanotechnology.

Nanoscale components, such as zinc oxide and titanium dioxide, are utilised in sunscreen lotions to provide more effective protection from the skin-aging effects of ultraviolet (UV) radiation.

Nanoscale delivery methods in skin care products can increase the efficacy of their active components by allowing them to penetrate deeper into the skin.

Products marketed as anti-aging often include nanoscale components intended to improve the look and feel of skin.

Fabrics and textiles are ten.

The following are some of the ways in which nanotechnology is influencing the textile and apparel industries:

Nanocoatings can be applied to fabrics to make them stain-resistant, which increases their longevity and enhances their aesthetic appeal.

More comfortable outdoor apparel is possible because to advances in nanotechnology that make materials both water- and air-repellent without sacrificing breathability.

- Antimicrobial fabrics: Thanks to advancements in nanotechnology, antimicrobial fabrics can now be produced, making them effective against odour and microbial growth.

Eleventh, Environmental Protection through Observation

Applications of nanotechnology for environmental monitoring and protection include:

Tiny, very sensitive nanosensors can detect and monitor environmental pollutants, helping to keep them below permissible levels and giving emergency responders access to real-time information.

Coatings made from nanomaterials can prevent environmental damage to buildings and bridges, elongating their useful life and decreasing the need for costly repairs.
Advanced wastewater treatment systems utilise nanotechnology for disinfection and pollutant removal to guarantee the safe discharge of effluent.

## 10.2- Economic and social implications of the nanotech revolution

The Impact of Nanotechnology on the Economy and Society.

The field of science known as nanotechnology is having far-reaching effects on our daily life and a number of different sectors. The economic and social effects of this cutting-edge technology are far-reaching, changing the way we work, live, and relate to one another and the world. This article will examine the effects of the nanotech revolution on economies and cultures around the world.

Economic Consequences

First, Innovating for Economic Growth

The advent of nanotechnology has spurred both productive activity and new ideas in the business world. It promotes innovation, new business formation, and financial activity across many industries. Using nanotechnology to create novel materials, goods, and processes has the potential to boost productivity, the economy, and the number of available jobs.

2. Impact on Multiple Industries

Electronics, medicine, energy, and manufacturing are just few of the many fields that can benefit from nanotechnology. These sectors become more efficient and competitive as they adopt nanotech applications. Nanotechnology's potential economic effects will be felt across industries, rather than just one.

Thirdly, International Rivalry

To stay ahead of the competition, countries are pouring resources into nanotechnology research and development. As a result, governments around the world are competing more than ever to be at the forefront of nanotechnology development. Such rivalry can spur economic expansion, but it also calls for just measures to bridge gaps in income and technology.

4. Expanded Market Potential

The nanotech revolution has created favourable conditions for the growth of new and creative firms. Entrepreneurs are capitalising on nanotechnology's promise to create ground-breaking new goods and services. The economic vitality and new job opportunities that result from this climate of enterprise are two of its many benefits.

5. Higher Productivity in the Factory

Manufacturing could be greatly improved with the use of nanotechnology. Improved manufacturing efficiency, less waste, and less production costs are all results of precision engineering and the creation of nanoscale materials. As a result, more competitiveness and profits can be expected from the economy.

Sixthly, Sustainability and Effective Use of Resources

One of the most important economic benefits of nanotechnology is the more effective use of resources. Nanotechnology paves the way for more efficient use of resources in fields like agriculture and energy. This helps sustainability efforts, cuts down on waste and carbon emissions, and improves financial results.

7. Patents and Other Forms of Intellectual Property

Intellectual property and patents play an important economic role with novel nanotech applications. To encourage creativity and protect creators' and businesses' financial interests, patenting innovative nanoscale innovations is crucial. This has sparked a flood of innovation-driven economic activity and a flurry of patent applications.

Risks to the Economy, Number 8

The economy could be vulnerable to the dangers posed by nanotechnology's rapid development. Disruption in markets, the loss of jobs, and inequalities in the use of new technologies are all difficulties for economies to overcome. There needs to be a plan in place to make sure the financial gains from nanotechnology trickle down to everyone and that any negative effects are contained.

Consequences for Society

Transformation in Health Care 1.

Nanotechnology is having a huge effect on the medical field. This is paving the way for preventative medicine, individualised treatment, and precise drug administration. This has positive effects on health, longevity, and quality of life. Healthier people who have easier access to high-quality medical treatment would have a positive impact on society.

2. Benefits to the Environment

Nanotechnology has serious consequences for the environment. It makes it easier to generate clean energy, purify water efficiently, and cut down on pollutants. Adopting nanotech solutions coincides with sustainable living practises, resulting in cleaner and healthier ecosystems, as societies become more environmentally conscious.

Thirdly, a Gap in Technology

The possibility for a technological divide is one of the social concerns posed by the nanotech revolution. Less developed countries may fall behind while more advanced ones engage extensively in nanotechnology R&D. If this divide isn't closed, it could make existing societal inequities much worse.

Scholastic Prospects 4.

Opportunities for advanced training in nanotechnology provide people with access to cutting-edge information and expertise. Nanotechnology and nanoscience education programmes result in a more qualified labour force, which benefits the economy as a whole. To ensure a workforce prepared to fully take advantage of the nanotech revolution, it is crucial that educational institutions evolve to provide training in nanotechnology.

5. Enhancing the Capacity of Neighbourhoods

Small-scale and community-based solutions are made possible by nanotechnology. Improvements in water purification, renewable energy generation, and medical treatment all help communities. The health and wealth of the community as a whole could benefit from such decentralisation of power.

Ethical Concerns 6.

Ethical questions raised by the rapid development of nanotechnology must be addressed by civilised groups. Because nanotechnology can be used for both good and evil, it is important to keep in mind the potential risks associated with it. Responsible research, sharing of technologies, and taking responsibility are all examples of ethical concerns.

Seventhly, Safety and Health

A major public worry is how nanotechnology will affect people's health and safety. Concerns regarding nanoparticles' potential dangers to scientists, workers, and consumers have been raised due to their unusual features. It is of the utmost importance to guarantee worker and consumer safety in settings where nanomaterials are used.8. Security and Privacy Nanotechnology's part in developing more compact and potent electrical components has prompted security and privacy worries. Society must deal with data protection, surveillance, and cybersecurity challenges as devices and sensors become increasingly prevalent. The Consumer Market and Public Understanding

Nanotechnology is increasingly widely used in consumer goods, often without the knowledge of the general public. The implication for society is the need to increase public awareness of nanotechnology's prevalence in consumer goods such as cosmetics, clothing, and electronics. With this knowledge, shoppers may make better decisions regarding the things they buy.

Tenth, Ecological Accountability

Nanotechnology has the potential to address environmental issues, however there are concerns about unintended consequences that need to be addressed. To reduce potential risks and assure the long-term viability of nanotechnology, society must prioritise nvironmental stewardship in its research, development, and lementation.Directions for the Future and Current Challenges

The nanotech revolution will have far-reaching effects on our economy and society, with enormous opportunities for improvement. There are, however, a number of obstacles to think about in light of these consequences. The longevity of the nanotech revolution depends on striking a balance between economic development and social and environmental responsibility. Nanotechnology holds great promise for improving lives and ensuring a sustainable future, but only if policymakers, scientists, and the general public work together to fully realise this potential.

www.ingramcontent.com/pod-product-compliance
Lightning Source LLC
LaVergne TN
LVHW020450070526
838199LV00063B/4900